LINDA McCARTNEY'S FAMILY KITCHEN

LINDA McCARTNEY

WITH PAUL, MARY & STELLA McCARTNEY

LINDA McCARTNEY'S FAMILY KITCHEN

OVER 90 PLANT-BASED RECIPES TO SAVE
THE PLANET AND NOURISH THE SOUL

SEVEN DIALS

Dedicated to our fellow creatures
living on this beautiful earth –
the animals.

CONTENTS

INTRODUCTION

by Paul McCartney

Becoming veggie was – and still is – hugely important to me and my family and I can't believe how much things have changed since we first gave up meat. Back in the day, vegetarians were viewed as a bit weird, and what veggie food you could find was stodgy and boring. Today, plant-based eating is massive and it's all about going vegan, not just vegetarian. I know that if Linda was with us now, she would love this plant-based revolution, and that's why we decided to take a fresh look at her legacy and her recipes and produce this book.

So why did our family decide to become vegetarian all that time ago? Linda and her family had always eaten meat and I'd been brought up on very traditional British food. The centre of a meal in our house when I was growing up was meat – a chop, maybe, or a couple of sausages – with some potatoes and perhaps a bit of veg on the side, and I continued to eat meat as an adult. But one day, Linda and I were having Sunday lunch with the family at our farm in Scotland and gazing out of the window at the baby lambs in the fields nearby. We were saying how cute and beautiful they were, then we looked at our plates. We were eating leg of lamb. We were eating one of those little things running around happily outside. That was the turning point for us and that's how it all started. For Linda, being vegetarian was first and foremost an act of kindness and compassion – it was about the animals. Any animal we saw, she would love – even a creepy little frog. In fact, one of the things we always shared was a huge passion for nature.

Our children were all quite young at the time, but we sat them down and talked about it. Our daughter Mary remembers Linda and I saying that we'd decided not to eat meat because we didn't want anything to suffer to be on our plate. We told the kids that they didn't have to become vegetarian too, but we wouldn't be cooking meat at home any more. It was fine – there wasn't any resentment. No one found it difficult. There was a near glitch a while later when we were on holiday in the Caribbean and we went to a barbecue. The kids were saying, 'Daddy, there's chicken. Can we have chicken?' And we said, 'Yeah, try it. But remember it's those birds we have in the yard at home.' They ate some chicken and didn't like it. That was a blessing. And to this day, all the children – and their children – are vegetarian.

At first, the thing for us was working out what we were going to eat, now that there was what we called that 'hole on the plate' where the meat used to be. We had lots of fun thinking up new dishes. Then Christmas came. Obviously, we didn't want to kill a turkey, so Linda came up with a brilliant idea – macaroni turkey! We made a big mound of mac 'n' cheese, left it to cool, then sliced it so it took the place of turkey on the plate. Then we added all the trimmings – roast potatoes, cranberry sauce and so on. Linda cooked them all amazingly, of course. Also, having the macaroni 'turkey' still allowed me that traditional male role of carver. I wanted to do that because it was the tradition. I wasn't being sexist. I just liked the idea, and it didn't matter to me that I was slicing mac 'n' cheese, not a turkey.

What's more, everything that Linda cooked was delicious; her main aim was always to make food taste great. That was important, because if a veggie meal wasn't that good, you might ask yourself: But why should I be veggie? This was never a problem for us.

The idea of starting a food company came later on. We'd be travelling back from Scotland to London or somewhere and would find ourselves hungry, so we'd call in at a stop-off.But there would never be much for us to eat. It was the same everywhere. Even in London I can only recall one vegetarian restaurant – Cranks. Just the name tells you what most people thought about vegetarian cooking at that time! So, Linda decided to do something about it. She said, 'Being compassionate means we'll be saving animals. If we make burgers out of plants, lots of cows will be saved.'

The business became very successful, but Linda wasn't in it for the money. She wanted to do some good and to help people get into vegetarian eating. Parents would write to her, saying that their children wanted to go veggie and they didn't know what to give them to eat. Linda's burgers and sausages helped them fill that gap where the meat had been.

Once Linda had the food business it was a natural follow-on for her to do a cookbook and she wrote her first one, *Home Cooking*, with food writer Peter Cox. It was fun to do, but for Peter the problem was that when he'd come to the house to watch Linda cook, she'd be putting in a bit of this and a bit of that and he had to keep stopping her to ask about weights and measures. She was such an instinctive cook. She'd had no training and had just learned by hanging out in the kitchen as a kid and watching the family's cook prepare meals. She just made what she liked to eat, and she wasn't afraid to experiment and try new things. Having to measure stuff was quite frustrating for her, but she did it because she wanted to spread the word.

Linda was very good at talking about being vegetarian. If we were at a dinner and someone was eating meat, she might call them out on it – but in a charming way. I couldn't do that. If I tried, it would get a bit messy and awkward. Linda was forthright, yet had the knack of persuading people gracefully and gently. The last thing we ever wanted to do was to alienate anyone by lecturing them, and Linda never did that. She had something magical. She was one of the pioneers of vegetarianism and the movement today owes a lot to her.

In 2006, eight years after Linda had died, I read a report from the United Nations. It was called Livestock's Long Shadow, and one of the things it revealed was that the livestock industry releases more greenhouse gases than transport does. Up until then I'd always thought transport was the big thing, but of course the livestock industry involves transport anyway. This added a great bonus to being vegetarian – I realised that not only was it about compassion and saving animals but also saving yourself, your kids, your grandkids; saving the world.

Up until then my feelings about vegetarianism were more about the animals, but after reading that report I realised there was more to it. There will be a huge ecological benefit if we change the way we eat and this is becoming more urgent by the day. So, the last chapter of our story was meat-free Monday – a campaign to raise awareness of the incredible impact of animal agriculture on the world. I'd heard of the idea, which was already in existence in the US, and thought: wow, we should do that. Mary, Stella and I got together a bunch of people and started to campaign and it really interested everyone. People who felt they couldn't go totally veggie thought: yeah, I could do that for a day, that's doable. And that's what we were aiming for. We didn't want people to think that eating less meat was too difficult. The word went around and it all started to happen without us having to be militant about it.

The thing I love now is that the vegetarian and vegan movement has taken on a momentum of its own, and I observe it with joy. The last time I was in New York, I went with my wife Nancy and her son – who is not a vegetarian – to a restaurant run by Jean-Georges Vongerichten, a really famous chef. He has a renowned restaurant called ABC Kitchen, and now, right next door, he has opened a superb vegetarian/vegan place – ABCV. It was like I was in heaven. The crowd in there was very cool – lots of young people and you felt you were among friends. The waiters were super friendly and helpful, and the food was amazing. I said to Nancy and Arlen that they couldn't know how incredible all this felt for me – that this was happening. I met the chef and he was adamant that the future is plant- based. I'm so glad he's saying that.

All the research says you can feed 20 times the number of people if you eat plant food direct instead of through an animal. So that's it – it's fantastic. True to Linda's stance, veggie food and vegan food are now everywhere, even in fast-food chains. I read somewhere that Burger King do a 'beyond meat burger' that outsells the regular burger and I like that because if there's business sense behind the movement, it will continue. It's not elitist.

We love to remember and promote Linda's work. We've done this with her photography and now the time has come to take a fresh look at her cooking legacy and her recipes. As a family, we are guardians of her food brand, Linda McCartney Foods, which is proudly entering its 30th year.

Linda was never one to get stuck in a rut and, if she was cooking today, she would be so thrilled to see all the great ingredients that are now so readily available – things like quinoa, tofu and so on. She would love all the ranges of plant-based products like oat milk and yoghurt, non-dairy butter and cheese, plant-based ice cream – cooking has become a whole different world. Being vegetarian and vegan is so easy now and so rewarding; and Linda was one of the pioneers who led to this. I'm so proud of her and all that she did. As chef Jean-Georges said: the future of food is plant-based and that, for me, is a cause for great celebration.

Paul

PLANT-BASED EATING

THE BEST WAY TO EAT

Some years ago, the American food writer Michael Pollan gave the best advice ever on eating: eat food, not too much, mostly plants. And he is so right. Plant-based eating celebrates the best nature has to offer without damaging the environment or killing or exploiting animals. It gets a big thumbs up from dieticians and nutritionists around the world, who agree it is the way forward in terms of our health – and the health of our planet. And most of all you'll eat the most delicious and satisfying meals.

Choosing plant-based food is a compassionate step that helps prevent cruelty and suffering. Think about the billions of animals that are slaughtered for their meat each year. Many are raised in factory farms in very cramped, overcrowded conditions with no access to daylight or fresh air. They are subjected to mutilations, such as having their beaks clipped, their teeth pulled out and tails docked to stop them from pecking and wounding each other through boredom and frustration.

Furthermore, the Food and Agriculture Organization of the United Nations estimates that livestock production is responsible for a whopping 14.5 per cent of global greenhouse gas emissions. Some studies suggest this puts livestock production on a par with transport in terms of the damage it is doing to our environment.

A 2020 Oxford University study found that, even if harmful greenhouse gas emissions from fossil fuels were to be stopped immediately, it would be impossible to keep global heating to the lowest safe limit without a shift to a more plant-based diet.

If you care about the environment, animal welfare and your health, adopting a plant-based way of eating makes perfect sense. You will be helping to slow climate change and protect the environment – and you'll live a healthier, happier life.

A plant-based diet is lower in saturated fat and higher in fibre, fruit and vegetables, wholegrains, pulses, nut and seeds. It's been shown, time and time again, to reduce the rate of heart disease, strokes, type 2 diabetes, high blood pressure, certain types of cancer and many other chronic diseases that are common in the western world.

WHAT TO EAT

Linda was a trailblazer for plant-based eating and it is now so much easier than when she wrote her first cookbooks. All the ingredients you need for tasty, healthy, plant-based meals are available in even the smallest supermarkets. Farmers' markets and box schemes make it possible to eat locally and seasonally, and as more and more people embrace plant-based eating, the range of plant-based and vegan alternatives is growing fast.

You don't have to give up the dishes you love. Enjoy your cup of tea or coffee with plant-based milk, have a delicious tofu scramble for breakfast, and make shepherd's pie with vegan mince or lentils. Fantastic burgers can be made with jackfruit and you can even whip up glorious cakes using soaked flax seeds instead of eggs.

If you're short of time there are plenty of healthy convenience foods such as canned beans, sauces, marinated tofu, sprouted seeds and even plant-based ready-meals and snacks that will help you put together a good meal in a matter of minutes. However, if you've bought this book and you're interested in doing the best for your health and wellbeing, you probably enjoy cooking great food. One of the main advantages of cooking from scratch is that you know exactly what's gone into the food you make and you have control over what you're eating. You'll probably save money too, as plant-based food is generally cheaper than animal protein.

A healthy plant-based meal should include food from each of these three food groups:

1. Vegetables and fruit

Aim to eat eight to ten portions a day. Fresh, frozen, canned all count.

2. Plant-based protein-rich foods

Protein-rich foods include beans, chickpeas, lentils, quinoa, nuts, seeds, nut butters, and soya products, such as tofu, soya milk, tempeh and edamame.

3. Starchy carbs

These include potatoes, pasta, rice, barley, noodles, oats, couscous, bulgur wheat, farro and polenta. Choose wholegrain carbs whenever possible.

In addition to these main food groups, include:

- Healthy fats such as extra virgin olive oil, rapeseed, walnut or flaxseed oil.
- At least two servings of calcium-rich foods (see page 18).

WHAT YOUR BODY NEEDS

Whatever your age or stage of life, a plant-based diet is the best way to nourish and protect your body. It's more than capable of meeting all your nutritional needs, but there are some key nutrients that you should make sure your diet provides.

Calcium

- Calcium is important for healthy strong bones throughout life but particularly while bones are still growing, which is until around the age of 25.

- If you like tofu, choose calcium-set tofu (look for calcium sulphate in the ingredients list); 100g of calcium-set tofu provides about 400mg of calcium, which is around half the daily requirement.

- The best way to ensure you're getting enough calcium is to eat two servings of calcium-rich food a day, such as 70g of calcium-set tofu, 200ml of calcium-fortified plant-based milk, two slices of soya and linseed bread fortified with calcium, or 200mg of calcium-fortified plant-based yoghurt.

- Other foods that help boost your calcium intake include almonds, sesame seeds, chia seeds, figs, peas, okra, red kidney beans, chickpeas, kale, broccoli, watercress, spring greens and tahini.

Omega-3 fatty acids

- Omega-3 fatty acids help to keep the heart and the brain healthy. You can get omega-3 fats from walnuts, flaxseed (linseeds), hemp seeds, chia seeds, rapeseed, algal and soya bean oil.

- A diet that is high in omega-6 fats, found in processed foods and vegetable oils, such as sunflower, safflower and corn oil, can stop the body from absorbing omega-3 fats, so replace those oils with healthier oils like extra virgin olive oil, rapeseed, linseed, walnut or soya bean oil.

Vitamin D

- Vitamin D is needed to keep bones, teeth and muscles healthy. Recent research suggests it's also vital for a healthy immune system.

- Plant-based sources include mushrooms and fortified foods like plant-based milk and spreads, but it can be difficult to get enough from your diet. Although the body can make vitamin D from the exposure of skin to sunlight, in the winter months it's not possible for the body to make enough. Health experts recommend that everyone should take a daily supplement of 10mg from October to late March.

- Always check the label on supplements before you buy because they're not always suitable for vegetarians and vegans.

Vitamin B12

- Vitamin B12 helps to keep the nervous system healthy and is needed by the body to make red blood cells.

- Many vegan foods, such as nutritional yeast, are fortified with B12. If you eat fortified foods, getting enough B12 in your diet isn't a problem.

- The Vegan Society recommends that you should eat a food fortified with B12 at each meal or take a supplement that contains at least 10mg of B12 each day.

Iodine

- The body needs iodine to make thyroid hormones, which regulate the speed at which your body burns calories. It's also essential for the development of a baby's brain during pregnancy and early life.

- You can get iodine from plant-based foods like spring greens, kale, watercress and green beans, but the iodine content depends on the iodine content of the soil in which the plants are grown. Seaweed can be a good source of iodine, but some types of seaweed, such as kelp, contain very high levels so it's best not to eat too much. Pregnant women are advised to avoid kelp and not to eat seaweed more than once a week.

Zinc

- Zinc is needed for growth, fertility, wound healing and a healthy immune system. Plant-based foods that provide a good amount of zinc include nuts and seeds, pulses, peas, tempeh and miso.

- It's easier for the body to absorb zinc from peas, beans and seeds that have been sprouted.

Selenium

- Selenium is needed for a healthy immune system; some studies show it may also help to reduce the risk of certain types of cancer.

- The amount of selenium in food depends on how much is in the soil in which the food is grown.

- Plant-based source of selenium include grains, nuts and seeds. Just two brazil nuts a day will provide you with your daily requirement.

Iron

- Iron is essential for the manufacture of red blood cells, which carry oxygen around the body, so it is hugely important for our energy levels.

- Plant-based sources of iron include dried fruit, green leafy vegetables like kale, cabbage and broccoli, nuts, chickpeas, kidney beans and lentils. Some breakfast cereals are fortified with iron.

- Vitamin C boosts the absorption of iron, so eat plenty of fruit and veg, which are rich in vitamin C, at the same time as your iron-rich foods.

USEFUL INGREDIENTS

Fridge

There's a wide range of plant-based milks, such as oat, coconut, soya, almond, so choose what you prefer. Just check that whatever you buy is unsweetened and look for calcium-fortified milk. Plant-based yoghurt, cream and crème fraîche are also useful – again, check that they are unsweetened. You may like dairy-free spread and cheese, and tofu and vegan mince are useful standbys.

Freezer

Frozen vegetables, such as peas, sweetcorn and edamame beans, are essentials. Throw a handful into stews or stir-fries and you'll be adding nutrients and fibre as well as flavour. Frozen berries are great for quick puddings and frozen ready-made pastry is a real time-saver.

Flour and baking ingredients

Stock up on dried yeast, baking powder and your choice of flour. Plain flour is fine or try spelt, which has a nice nutty flavour. If you have a gluten intolerance, go for gluten-free flour or, for some recipes, you can use buckwheat or gram (chickpea flour).

Nuts, nut butters and seeds

Nuts are such a useful food: add them to salads or bakes, or just enjoy them as a nutritious snack. Seeds such as flaxseeds (linseeds), sesame, pumpkin and hemp add nutrients and flavour to dishes and make good snacks. Nut butters are great in bakes or spread on crackers, oatcakes or slices of apple as a quick energy booster.

Grains

If you keep a supply of grains, like oats, bulgur wheat and quinoa, as well as brown, basmati, risotto and jasmine rice in your cupboard you'll always be able to make a meal.

Pasta and noodles

Macaroni, lasagne, wholewheat pasta in shapes of your choice, noodles – soba, flat rice, vermicelli – again, great for a quick meal. Check that any pasta you buy is egg-free.

Oils and vinegars

We mostly use extra virgin olive oil, but you may like to have vegetable, sesame seed and coconut oils. Vinegars – apple cider, red wine, rice, balsamic – are all useful.

Sweetening agents

We've kept sugar to a minimum in these recipes, but we all like a sweet treat from time to time, so stock up on unrefined, caster, coconut palm, light brown and icing sugar. Maple syrup is great for pancakes.

Canned and dried

Tinned pulses, such as black-eyed beans, butter beans, black beans, haricot beans and chickpeas, as well as sachets of lentils, all keep for ages and it's great to have a few different kinds for quick meals. Keep some dried pulses too and cook up a batch when you have time, then freeze them for another day. Canned tomatoes, sweetcorn and passata are always useful. Dried fruit, such as medjool dates, ready-to-eat apricots, cranberries, raisins and sultanas, can be used in baking and puddings.

Seasonings, spices and condiments

You'll need stock cubes or powder, sea salt and black pepper. It's good to keep a collection of spices – cinnamon, smoked paprika, chilli flakes, coriander, cumin, turmeric, allspice and saffron all feature in the recipes in this book. Other useful items are miso, nutritional yeast, dried mixed herbs, tahini, mustard, sriracha sauce, soy sauce (or tamari for a gluten-free option), sweet chilli sauce, vegan mayonnaise, capers and gherkins.

TOP TIPS FOR ENJOYING
A PLANT-BASED DIET

Be adventurous

The more varied your diet, the more likely it is to be balanced and healthy (and enjoyable for you), so try new ingredients and recipes.

Different foods contain different nutrients and health-promoting compounds such as phytochemicals, but no single food or food group provides all the necessary nutrients. The best way to ensure your body gets everything it needs is to enjoy a variety of different foods. Eat the rainbow – make sure you have as many different coloured vegetables as possible, such as orange carrots, purple beetroot, yellow peppers, red tomatoes as well as greens, Nutritionists suggest you aim to have around 30 different plant-based foods every week so that you get a good range of nutrients and maintain great gut health.

Fill up with fibre

Fibre-rich foods are essential for a healthy system. NHS guidelines say we should have about 30g of fibre a day, but most people only average about 18g a day. Eating plenty of fibre helps us keep a healthy digestive system and also reduces the risk of heart disease, type 2 diabetes and bowel cancer. Fibre-rich foods include wholewheat cereals, oats, wholewheat bread and pasta, pulses, potatoes with their skins on, nuts, seeds, fruit such as berries, pears, melon and oranges, and vegetables such as broccoli, carrots and sweetcorn.

Plan ahead and shop wisely

Write a weekly meal plan. Take a little time at the weekend to plan what you will eat in the week ahead. This will help you check that your diet is balanced and includes all the nutrients your body needs. Try to buy local and seasonal ingredients to cut down on food miles.

Check the nutrition information on packaged and ready-prepared foods. Compare the salt, fat, sugar and fibre in different brands. Some processed plant-based foods contain a lot of additives, so check the ingredients list as well as the nutrition panel.

Keep your store cupboard, fridge and freezer stocked with healthy ingredients. Again, whatever type of diet you follow, it's much easier to put together healthy and delicious meals if you have a well-stocked kitchen. See page 20 for a list of ingredients you might need for the recipes in this book.

Follow healthy eating guidelines

Eat less salt and sugar, and choose wholegrain and fibre-rich carbs. Remember that 'natural' sugars such as agave, maple syrup, honey and coconut sugar are still sugar, so they should be limited.

COOK'S TIPS

Skinning tomatoes

Cut a cross in the top of each tomato, place in a heatproof bowl and cover with boiling water. Leave for a couple of minutes, then drain, rinse in cold water and slip off the skins.

Skinning peppers

Put the peppers on a baking tray and cook at 200°C/Fan 180°C/Gas 6 for 20–30 minutes, turning them from time to time until they have blackened all over. Place them in a paper bag and leave for 10 minutes, then the skins will peel off easily.

Preparing avocados

It's best to leave the preparation of avocados until just before you want to eat them, as the flesh will discolour.

1. Take a sharp knife and cut the avocado in half lengthways, cutting around the central stone

2. Twist the halves in opposite directions to separate them. Using a teaspoon, remove the stone from the centre.

3. Either peel off the skin and slice the flesh or scoop out the flesh with a spoon and mash it. To stop the avocado going brown, add lemon or lime juice or vinegar, or, for mashed avocado, put the stone in the centre until ready to serve. If not using the whole avocado, leave the stone in the remaining half and cover. It will keep in the fridge for a day.

Fresh herbs

It's good to always have some fresh herbs on hand. They're easy to grow from seed, so keep pots of your favourites on your kitchen windowsill. Fresh herbs freeze well too..

Check ingredients

If you're following a strict vegan diet, make sure that any wine you use is vegan friendly. And check the ingredients of sauces, pickles and so on. Use proper measuring equipment – scales, measuring jugs, teaspoons and tablespoons – but feel free to adapt recipes to your taste, adding more or less spice, for example.

Prep time and cook time

You'll see little icons on each recipe, giving guidelines on the time it takes to prepare and cook. Again, we've made these as accurate as possible but they will vary, depending on your knife skills and your oven.

"I HAVE A PASSION FOR PEACE AND I BELIEVE IT STARTS WITH COMPASSION TO ANIMALS"

BREAKFAST AND BRUNCH

AMERICAN-STYLE PANCAKES

Linda was renowned for making the most delicious, fluffy, American-style breakfast pancakes. This version of her recipe uses baking powder and apple cider vinegar to give the pancakes their lift. Drizzle with maple syrup and add a handful of fresh berries for breakfast perfection.

SERVES 4–6
(MAKES 16 PANCAKES)

280g plain flour

1½ tbsp baking powder

½ tsp fine sea salt

500ml unsweetened plant-based milk of your choice

2 tbsp apple cider vinegar

2 tsp vanilla extract

1 tbsp olive oil

Vegetable oil, to fry

To serve

200g berries of your choice

Maple syrup

Sift the flour into a large mixing bowl, then stir in the baking powder and salt and mix everything together. Pour the plant milk into a measuring jug, then add the cider vinegar and vanilla. Gradually mix the liquid into the dry ingredients until smooth. Finally, stir in the olive oil.

Heat a tablespoon of vegetable oil in a large non-stick frying pan and place over a medium heat. Once the oil is hot, add 4 tablespoons of batter per pancake, taking care not to overcrowd the pan. Fry the pancakes for 2–3 minutes on one side, until bubbles appear on the surface, then flip them over and fry for another minute or so until both sides are golden. Keep the pancakes warm in a low oven while you fry the rest in batches, adding more oil as needed. You could use a second frying pan if you want to speed up the process.

Serve the pancakes immediately with the berries and some maple syrup drizzled over the top.

PREP
15

COOK
35

WEEKEND BRUNCH

This hearty breakfast of turmeric- and garlic-scrambled tofu, veggie sausages, baked beans and toast is so satisfying and delicious. Perfect with the home-made baked beans on page 30 if you have the time, but shop-bought also work wonderfully.

SERVES 2

200g cherry tomatoes

4 tbsp extra virgin olive oil

4 Linda McCartney
vegetarian sausages, or
others of your choice

400g firm tofu, drained

1 medium garlic clove,
peeled and finely chopped

½ tsp ground turmeric

100ml vegetable stock

200g portobello mushrooms,
thickly sliced, or baby
portobellos

200g baked beans (see p.30
or shop-bought)

Sea salt and freshly ground
black pepper, to taste

To serve

Toast

Preheat the oven to 200°C/Fan 180°C/Gas 6.

Put the tomatoes on one side of a large baking tray, drizzle them with a tablespoon of the olive oil and season generously with salt and pepper. Put the sausages on the other side of the tray and cover with foil so the sausages don't dry out. Place the tray in the oven for about 16 minutes, until the tomatoes have almost burst open and the sausages are cooked through.

Meanwhile, tightly wrap the tofu in a clean tea towel and, holding it over a sink, squeeze out as much liquid as possible. Heat a tablespoon of the oil in a large non-stick frying pan over a medium-high heat. Add the tofu and stir-fry for 4–5 minutes until golden, while breaking it up with the back of a spoon. Add the garlic, turmeric and stock and fry for another 3–5 minutes, stirring now and again, until the stock has reduced, and you are left with soft, scrambled tofu. Season to taste with salt and pepper.

Place another large frying pan over a high heat and add the remaining 2 tablespoons of oil. Once the pan is very hot, add the mushrooms and fry them for 6–8 minutes until softened and golden. Season to taste.

Heat the beans in a saucepan over a medium-low heat. Plate up the tomatoes, sausages, scrambled tofu, mushrooms and beans and serve immediately with toast.

BAKED BEANS

These baked beans are warming, comforting and nourishing, and by making your own you are in control of exactly what's in them – all good stuff and no additives. They're also great on a baked potato for lunch or dinner.

SERVES 6

2 tbsp extra virgin olive oil

1 medium onion, peeled and finely chopped

2 medium garlic cloves, peeled and crushed

1 tsp sweet smoked paprika

2 x 400g tins of haricot beans, drained and rinsed

600g tomato passata

2 tbsp maple syrup

2 tbsp red wine vinegar

Sea salt and freshly ground black pepper, to taste

To serve

Toast

Add the oil to a medium-sized pan and place it over a medium heat. Stir in the onion and fry gently for 8–10 minutes until soft, but not coloured. Then add the garlic and paprika and fry for 2 minutes until you smell the aroma. Add the remaining ingredients and a teaspoon of salt and bring to the boil.

Reduce the heat to low and simmer gently for 30 minutes, stirring now and again, until the mixture has thickened. Season generously with salt and pepper and add a little more maple syrup or red wine vinegar to taste.

Serve with toast, on a baked potato, or as part of a weekend brunch.

HASH BROWNS

Another nod to Linda's American heritage, hash browns have always been a family favourite. This recipe includes carrot as well as potato for a little extra flavour, and if you want a bit of spice add some chilli or cumin to taste.

SERVES 4

2 tbsp extra virgin olive oil, plus extra to grease

375g floury potatoes, such as Maris Pipers or King Edwards, washed and coarsely grated (no need to peel)

125g carrots, peeled and coarsely grated

½ medium onion, peeled, halved and very thinly sliced

1 tbsp cornflour

Sea salt and freshly ground black pepper, to taste

Preheat the oven to 190°C/Fan 170°C/Gas 5. Line a large baking tray with baking paper and lightly grease it with olive oil.

Place the grated potatoes and carrots in the centre of a clean tea towel. Wrap the tea towel tightly around the grated vegetables and squeeze out as much liquid as possible over a sink. Transfer the potatoes and carrots to a large bowl and combine with the onion, 2 tablespoons of olive oil, the cornflour, three-quarters of a teaspoon of salt and half a teaspoon of black pepper.

Divide the mixture into 12 portions of equal size, about 45g each. Take each portion and gently compact it together with your hands, then flatten it into a round and carefully place it on the baking tray.

Bake for 20 minutes, then increase the heat to 220°C/Fan 200°C/Gas 7 and continue to cook for another 6–10 minutes, until deeply golden brown and crispy. Remove the hash browns from the oven and leave to cool for a couple of minutes, then season with a little more salt and pepper. Serve immediately on their own or with the tofu scramble (p.46) or brunch spread (p.28).

"

WHEN I WAS A CHILD
I LOVED ANIMALS TO
THE POINT WHERE MY
PARENTS WONDERED
ABOUT ME. I WOULD
SAVE A SQUIRREL,
I WOULD BRING
HOME A CHIPMUNK, A
WOUNDED BIRD, AND
I'D TAKE CARE OF THEM.

"

Linda McCartney – 1991

BLUEBERRY AND BANANA
BREAKFAST MUFFINS

Muffins, a classic brunch staple, are also great with a cup of tea or coffee at any time of day. These contain cider vinegar and baking powder to make them rise and we love them. They're bursting with goodness and lively blueberry flavour. The berries are an excellent source of vitamin C, while bananas are rich in potassium.

MAKES 8 MUFFINS

140g white spelt or
plain flour

½ tsp bicarbonate of soda

½ tsp baking powder

½ tsp sea salt

35g rolled oats

1 ripe banana, peeled
and mashed

1 tsp vanilla extract

120ml unsweetened plant-
based milk of your choice

80ml maple syrup

2 tsp apple cider vinegar

150g blueberries

Preheat the oven to 200°C/Fan 180°C/Gas 6. Line a muffin tray with 8 paper cases.

In a large bowl, mix the flour, bicarbonate of soda, baking powder, salt and most of the oats – set aside about a tablespoon of oats for topping the muffins.

In a separate bowl, combine the mashed banana, vanilla extract, milk, maple syrup, vinegar and most of the blueberries – reserve a tablespoon of berries for the topping. Add the banana mixture to the flour mixture and mix everything together.

Divide the mixture evenly between the paper cases, then sprinkle with the reserved oats and blueberries. Bake the muffins for 20–25 minutes, until a skewer comes out mostly clean. Remove them from the oven and leave to cool on a wire rack before serving.

BIRCHER MUESLI POTS

A classic bircher muesli with some added extras, such as crunchy pumpkin seeds, dried fruit and a little spice, together with some non-dairy yoghurt and milk, makes a yummy and nutritious breakfast. Allow for soaking time when making this – three hours or overnight, ready for a delicious breakfast the next day.

SERVES 4

150g rolled oats
   (preferably jumbo)

1 apple, cored and grated

150ml unsweetened plant-
   based milk of your choice

150ml fresh orange or
   apple juice

40g dried fruit, such
   as raisins, cranberries
   or apricots, plus extra
   to serve

40g pumpkin seeds

1 tsp ground cinnamon

200g non-dairy yoghurt

To serve

40g roasted blanched
   hazelnuts (or other
   nuts of your choice)

Seasonal fruit of your
   choice

In a large bowl, mix together all the ingredients, except the nuts and fresh fruit. Divide the mixture between 4 large jam jars or containers, cover and leave to soak for at least 3 hours or preferably overnight in the fridge.

Serve with the hazelnuts scattered over the top and fresh fruit.

PREP
10

COOK
10

FRENCH TOAST

Quick and easy, French toast was a favourite treat when we were children and we still love it today. Linda used the irresistible flavours of cinnamon, vanilla and maple syrup in her recipe and, when topped with fruit for a burst of juiciness, this makes a really luxurious special breakfast. It's the perfect way to use up slightly stale bread.

SERVES 6

3 tbsp plain or gram (chickpea) flour

370ml unsweetened plant-based milk of your choice

2 tbsp maple syrup, plus extra to drizzle

2 tsp vanilla extract

2 tsp ground cinnamon

6 thick slices of soft wholegrain, white or gluten-free bread

Coconut oil, to fry

To serve

Non-dairy yoghurt

Almond butter, to drizzle

Seasonal fruit of your choice, such as figs, berries, mango

In a bowl, whisk together the flour, milk, maple syrup, vanilla extract and cinnamon until thoroughly combined, ensuring there are no lumps. Pour the mixture into a wide flat dish. One by one, dip the slices of bread into the mixture, leaving them for 10–15 seconds on each side, so they are soft but not falling apart.

Put a teaspoon of the coconut oil into a large non-stick frying pan and place over a medium-high heat. Once the oil is hot, add 2 or 3 slices of bread and fry them for 3–4 minutes on each side, until golden and slightly crispy. Cook the remaining bread in the same way, adding more coconut oil as needed.

Serve the French toast topped with the yoghurt, almond butter and fruit, and drizzle over some more maple syrup.

I remember Mum and Dad sitting us down and saying they had something to talk to us about. And that was when they explained that they'd decided not to eat meat any longer, as they didn't want any creature to suffer in order to be on our plates. They said that we children didn't have to be vegetarian, but they wouldn't be cooking meat at home any longer.

It turned out that it was fine with us. We still had great home-cooked food and we felt like we had a chance to talk about it all and make our own decisions as time progressed. We liked discussing and deciding how to fill what we called the 'hole on the plate' – the space left when you stop eating meat or fish – so you didn't feel you were just eating side orders. In the end, what everyone wants is nice food that you feel good about and that you know doesn't have a negative impact on the planet.

When we were kids we all helped in the kitchen and it was definitely the hub of our home – the favourite room in the house. Mum liked company – quite rightly, she didn't want to be in there cooking all on her own. There was always something going on in our kitchen and we had a big table where you could sit and chop and peel or just talk.

Mary

SWEET POTATO RÖSTI WITH AVOCADO, CORIANDER AND CHILLI

Packed with flavour and so moreish, sweet potatoes are a great source of minerals and vitamins, particularly C and E. They are also rich in fibre, which is great for the digestive system. And all the veggies in this count towards your five a day.

SERVES 4

600g sweet potato, peeled

1 medium red onion, peeled and very finely chopped

2 medium garlic cloves, peeled and crushed

1 tsp cumin seeds or ground cumin

1 tsp ground coriander

½ tsp ground cinnamon

5 tbsp gram (chickpea) flour or plain white flour

4 tbsp extra virgin olive oil, plus extra to fry

Sea salt and freshly ground black pepper, to taste

To serve

2 ripe avocados

Chopped coriander leaves

1 red chilli, deseeded and thinly sliced

Lime wedges (optional)

Coarsely grate the sweet potato. Place it in the centre of a clean tea towel, roll the towel up and squeeze out as much liquid as possible over a sink, twisting the towel as you go.

Tip the sweet potato into a bowl and mix with the red onion, garlic, cumin, coriander, cinnamon, flour and 4 tablespoons of olive oil. Season with 2 teaspoons of salt and half a teaspoon of black pepper, then use clean hands to bring everything together.

Add a tablespoon of oil to a large non-stick pan and place it over a medium-low heat. Take 2 tablespoons of the sweet potato mixture in your hand and tightly compact it into a ball, then gently flatten it into a disc and place it in the hot pan. Repeat with more of the mixture, taking care not to overcrowd the pan. Fry the rösti for 4–5 minutes until golden on one side, then gently flip over and fry for another 4–5 minutes, until golden and cooked through. Transfer to a plate and continue until you've used all the mixture, adding more oil as needed.

Halve the avocados, remove the stones and slice the flesh. Plate up the rösti and avocado, season and scatter over the coriander leaves and chilli. Drizzle with a little more olive oil and serve immediately with lime wedges if desired.

PREP
10

COOK
30

TOFU SCRAMBLE WITH BAKED
TOMATOES AND WILTED SPINACH

One of the most effective ways to reduce your carbon footprint is to move to a plant-based diet. This is a breakfast feast that tastes fabulous and does you good. It's low in fat and high in nutrients, so it's the perfect way to start the day.

SERVES 2

2 large ripe tomatoes,
    halved

½ tsp sugar

300g firm tofu

1 tbsp extra virgin olive oil,
    plus extra to drizzle

4 spring onions,
    finely chopped

2 medium garlic cloves,
    peeled and crushed

¼ tsp sweet
    smoked paprika

½ tsp ground turmeric

125ml unsweetened plant-
    based milk of your choice

250g baby spinach, washed

Sea salt and freshly ground
    black pepper, to taste

To serve

2 slices of sourdough bread

Preheat the oven to 200°C/Fan 180°C/Gas 6. Place the halved tomatoes on a baking tray, cut-side up, season to taste with sea salt and pepper and sprinkle over the sugar. This helps the tomatoes to caramelise. Place them in the oven for 20 minutes, until bubbling and golden.

Tightly wrap a clean tea towel around the tofu. Over a sink, squeeze the tofu very firmly to extract as much water as possible, almost wringing out the tofu. Unwrap the tofu and crumble it into a bowl, breaking up any larger pieces with a fork.

Heat the tablespoon of olive oil in a large pan over a medium heat. Add the spring onions and garlic, then fry gently for 2–3 minutes to soften. Add the paprika and turmeric and fry for a minute until aromatic. Add the tofu and stir well to combine. Then pour in the milk and simmer for 5–7 minutes, stirring now and again, until it has reduced and become creamy. Season generously with salt and pepper to taste. Tip into a bowl and keep warm.

Return the pan to the heat, add the spinach and cook for 1–2 minutes over a high heat, turning every now and then, until the spinach has wilted. Squeeze out any excess water, season well to taste and toss with a teaspoon of olive oil.

To serve, toast the sourdough bread, then drizzle with a little olive oil. Serve with the tofu scramble, spinach and baked tomatoes.

46   *Breakfast and Brunch*

CINNAMON ROLLS

The wonderful aroma of these rolls baking in the oven is guaranteed to make everyone's mouth water. They're soft and chewy and filled with delicious cinnamon butter. An ideal way to brighten the morning for you and the ones you love.

MAKES 12 ROLLS

Dough

100g non-dairy butter, splus extra to grease

400ml unsweetened plant-based milk of your choice, at room temperature, not chilled

40g unrefined or caster sugar

7g sachet of fast-action dried yeast

620g white spelt flour or plain white flour, plus extra to dust

1 tsp fine sea salt

Filling

140g non-dairy butter, softened

110g light brown sugar

1½ tbsp ground cinnamon

60g pecan nuts, finely chopped (optional)

Line a baking tray with baking paper and grease with a little non-dairy butter.

Melt the 100g of butter and put it in a large bowl with the plant milk, sugar and yeast. Mix together and leave aside for 5 minutes. Add the flour and salt and stir until just combined. Cover and set aside in a warm part of your kitchen for about an hour, or until doubled in size.

Dust the dough with 2 tablespoons of flour and knock out the air with your fist. Very generously dust your work surface with 3 or 4 tablespoons of flour (as it is a wet dough) and transfer the ball of dough to the surface. With floured hands to prevent sticking, bring the dough into a ball and roll it around on the floured surface so that all sides are coated in flour and not sticking to the surface at all. Knead gently for 1–2 minutes, dusting with more flour as needed to prevent any sticking. With a floured rolling pin, roll out the dough into a large thin, neat rectangle, just under 1cm thick. Spread the softened butter over the surface of the dough, then sprinkle over the sugar, cinnamon and nuts, if using, so they evenly cover the surface.

Starting from the longest side, tightly roll up the dough to form a log, with the seam facing down. Cut the log in half with a floured knife and then cut each half into 6 slices of equal thickness. Carefully transfer the rolls to the baking tray, so they are sitting snugly beside each other. Cover with cling film and set aside for another 30–40 minutes to rise. Preheat the oven to 180°C/Fan 160°C/Gas 4.

Icing

130g icing sugar, sifted

2 tbsp unsweetened plant-
    based milk of your choice

1½ tsp vanilla extract

Remove the cling film and bake the rolls for 25–30 minutes, until well risen and golden.

Meanwhile, for the icing, whisk together the icing sugar, milk and vanilla extract in a bowl until smooth. Once the rolls are cooked, remove them from the oven and leave to cool for 10 minutes, then drizzle over the icing and serve immediately.

BORSCHT SOUP

Rich and deep in colour, this beetroot soup is full of flavour and vitamins – and was a great favourite of Linda's. Serve it chunky or smooth – whatever you prefer. And if you buy fresh beets with their leaves attached, you can save the leaves and use them just as you would spinach.

SERVES 6–8

2 tbsp extra virgin olive oil, plus extra to drizzle

1 medium onion, peeled and finely chopped

600g medium beetroots, peeled and finely chopped

1 medium potato, peeled and finely chopped

250g Savoy or other cabbage, shredded

2 litres vegetable stock

2 tbsp fresh lemon juice

Sea salt and freshly ground black pepper, to taste

To serve

60g non-dairy crème fraîche or plain yoghurt

Chopped fresh parsley or dill

Put the oil in a large pan and place over a medium-high heat. Add the onion and sauté for 4 minutes until it begins to soften. Add the beetroot, potato and cabbage and fry for another 5 minutes. Season to taste with salt and black pepper.

Add the stock. Bring to the boil, then reduce the heat to medium and simmer gently for 20–30 minutes until everything is tender. Stir in the lemon juice and season to taste. Leave to cool for 10 minutes, then purée two-thirds of the soup in a blender and tip it back into the pan. You can purée it all if you want a smooth soup.

Reheat the soup and serve in bowls with a little crème fraîche or plain yoghurt on top. Scatter over the parsley or dill and add a little drizzle of olive oil.

TOMATO AND ROSEMARY SOUP

It was a family tradition that everyone got to choose their birthday meal, and this soup was often on the menu. It was based on a fantastic lobster bisque that Linda and Paul ate on a trip to the South of France, back in the days before we were vegetarian. Much later, Linda adapted it to make this incredible version that we still love.

SERVES 2–4

700g ripe tomatoes

2 tbsp extra virgin olive oil

1 medium onion, peeled and finely chopped

1 celery stick, finely chopped, tough strings removed

1 tbsp fresh rosemary, finely chopped

100ml vegetable stock

200g tomato passata

400ml unsweetened plant-based cream, ideally soya

Sea salt and freshly ground black pepper, to taste

To serve
Extra virgin olive oil
Basil leaves (optional)

First skin the tomatoes (see page 23). It is worth doing this, so you don't end up with little bits of skin in your otherwise silky soup. Cut the tomatoes into quarters.

Heat the oil in a large saucepan, add the onion, celery, rosemary and tomatoes and cook gently for 4 minutes. Then add the stock and passata and bring to the boil. Immediately reduce the heat and simmer gently for 15–20 minutes until the vegetables have softened. Season to taste. Leave to cool for 5 minutes, then purée in a food processor or with a stick blender until the soup is completely smooth. Gradually blend in the soya cream.

Reheat when ready to serve. Top with a little drizzle of olive oil and a few grinds of black pepper to taste. Garnish with a few basil leaves, if using.

PREP 25   COOK 1h15

MINESTRONE SOUP

Linda always loved Italian food and this gorgeous soup was a family favourite. With some good bread, it's a meal in itself and any leftovers keep well in the fridge or freezer.

SERVES 8

3 tbsp extra virgin olive oil

2 medium onions, peeled and finely chopped

2 celery sticks, thinly sliced, tough strings removed

2 medium carrots, peeled and finely chopped

2 medium garlic cloves, peeled and finely chopped

1 tbsp dried mixed herbs

400g tin of chopped tomatoes

1 tbsp tomato purée

2 medium courgettes, finely chopped

200g green cabbage, finely chopped

1 medium turnip, peeled and diced

1.6 litres vegetable stock

100g macaroni

400g tin of flageolet or haricot beans, drained and rinsed

Put the oil in a large pan with a lid and place over a medium heat. Add the onions, celery, carrots and a large pinch of salt and cook for 10 minutes until the vegetables are just beginning to soften. Add the garlic and mixed herbs and cook for another 2 minutes, until aromatic.

Add the chopped tomatoes, tomato purée, courgettes, cabbage and turnip, then the stock and cover with the lid. Simmer for 45 minutes until the vegetables are tender. Add the macaroni, beans and cooked diced potato – it helps to parboil the potato before adding it to the soup to avoid scum from the starch forming on the surface. Cook for a further 15 minutes until the pasta is al dente. Season to taste.

Serve in bowls with a drizzle of olive oil, parsley and some grated non-dairy cheese if you like.

150g potatoes, peeled,
 diced and parboiled

Sea salt and freshly ground
 black pepper, to taste

To serve

Extra virgin olive oil

Small bunch of flatleaf
 parsley, leaves only

40g non-dairy parmesan,
 grated (optional)

PREP
15

CHILLED AVOCADO AND CHILLI SOUP

This chilled soup is perfect on a hot summer's day and has a delicious creaminess to contrast with the kick of chilli – a winning combination. Avocados are an excellent source of essential fats, which makes them really satisfying to eat, and they are packed with vitamins, particularly vitamin E, and fibre. This is a great way to enjoy them.

SERVES 4

2 ripe avocados, halved, peeled and stones removed (see p.23)

700ml unsweetened plant-based milk, such as soya

1 small Spanish yellow onion, peeled and chopped, or 2 spring onions, chopped

1 medium garlic clove, peeled and crushed

2 pickled chillies or 1 fresh green or red chilli, deseeded and sliced, plus extra to serve

2½ tbsp fresh lemon or lime juice, plus extra to taste

Sea salt and freshly ground black pepper, to taste

To serve
Extra virgin olive oil
Sourdough bread

Put the avocado flesh and all of the remaining soup ingredients, except the seasoning, into a high-speed blender with 60ml of water. Blitz until completely smooth. Season generously to taste with salt, pepper and a little extra lemon or lime juice if required. If you prefer the soup a little thinner, stir in a little more water.

Serve at room temperature or refrigerate until well-chilled, if you prefer. To serve, divide the soup between bowls, scatter over some sliced chilli and add a drizzle of olive oil. This is nice with wedges of sourdough bread.

PREP
15

GAZPACHO WITH A TWIST

Linda's twist on the much-loved Spanish chilled soup is both super refreshing and fantastically tasty. Really ripe tomatoes give the best results and they also contain the most lycopene – a nutrient that is believed to help protect against heart disease. The optional addition of vegan mayo might be controversial but it adds a lovely creaminess.

SERVES 4

500g very ripe tomatoes

1 medium garlic
   clove, peeled

1 small red onion, peeled
   and roughly chopped, or
   4 spring onions, chopped

½ cucumber, roughly
   chopped

1 red pepper, deseeded
   and roughly chopped,
   or a few pimientos
   from a jar

1 tbsp red wine vinegar

1 tbsp vegan mayonnaise
   (optional)

2 tbsp extra virgin olive oil,
   plus extra to serve

4 basil leaves, plus
   extra to serve

¾ tsp sea salt

Large pinch of black
   pepper, plus extra
   to serve

Skin the tomatoes (see page 23) and chop them roughly. Place all the ingredients in a high-speed blender and blitz until completely smooth. Taste and adjust the seasoning with a little more vinegar and salt if necessary. Refrigerate the gazpacho for at least 2 hours, or until very well chilled.

When ready to serve, taste the gazpacho again to check for a good balance of tastes, as flavours dull when chilled. Divide between bowls, drizzle over a little olive oil and add some black pepper and a few basil leaves.

PREP
20

CHEF'S SALAD

Linda loved salads and this is nutritious and satisfying – a yummy meal in a bowl. The ingredients provide great crunch and bite, all tossed in a tangy dressing. Save the liquid from the chickpeas – known as aquafaba – for making the Eton mess on page 240. It keeps for several days in the fridge or can be frozen.

SERVES 4

200g baby gem lettuce

4 ripe tomatoes

175g cucumber

1 avocado, halved, peeled and stone removed (see p.23)

400g firm tofu of your choice, such as marinated or smoked

400g tin of chickpeas, drained and rinsed

Dressing

3½ tbsp apple cider vinegar

120ml extra virgin olive oil

2 tsp Dijon mustard

2 tsp maple syrup (optional)

1 medium garlic clove, peeled and crushed

Sea salt and freshly ground black pepper, to taste

Roughly chop the lettuce and place it in a large serving dish. Chop the tomatoes, cucumber, avocado and tofu into bite-sized pieces and add them and the chickpeas to the dish.

Put all the dressing ingredients into a bowl, whisk to combine and season to taste with salt and pepper – you will need at least half a teaspoon of salt. When you're ready to serve the salad, pour over the dressing and toss gently to combine.

I don't ever remember Mum following a recipe in a cookbook, which is funny considering that now, all these years on, we are revisiting her own recipes, from some of the most pioneering vegetarian cookbooks ever produced. Mum was one of those amazing natural cooks. She seemed to know exactly how long it took for a potato to boil or for broccoli to steam to perfection. She was a master at making salad dressings. We were never allowed to wash out the salad bowl because it was made from a solid piece of oak and might crack, so we would wipe it down and preserve all the dressing oil nutrients to keep it alive for many years and generations to come.

All of us can cook and it's from watching Mum. Kindness and care were in every meal and every mouthful. Like her, I love our fellow creatures and respect them, so I cook only plant-based meals. This really is soul food and Mum always used to say that she made food for the soul.

Stella

CRUNCHY COLESLAW

Bright, colourful and packed with vitamins and minerals, coleslaw livens up any meal. It can be made ahead of time and stored in an airtight container until needed. Linda would always make a tasty vinaigrette dressing to elevate coleslaw to something special.

SERVES 6
AS A SIDE DISH

500g red or white cabbage (or a mixture), very finely shredded

100g kale, stalks removed, and leaves shredded or very finely sliced

1 medium carrot, peeled and grated

Dressing

Zest of ½ lemon and 3 tbsp lemon juice

4 tbsp extra virgin olive oil

1 tbsp vegan mustard

1 tbsp red wine vinegar

Sea salt and freshly ground black pepper, to taste

In a large bowl, mix the cabbage, kale and carrot. Mix the lemon zest, juice, olive oil, mustard and vinegar to make the dressing, then season generously with salt and pepper to taste.

Mix the dressing with the salad and leave to chill in the fridge for 30 minutes before serving.

PREP 15   COOK 5

RADISH, BEAN AND FENNEL SALAD

In this sophisticated salad, the aniseedy taste of the finely sliced or shredded fennel goes beautifully with the peppery radishes. The inclusion of beans and the quinoa or rice makes this hearty and rich in protein too, while still gluten-free.

SERVES 4

4 tbsp extra virgin olive oil

2 medium garlic cloves, peeled and crushed

1 tsp ground cumin

1 tsp sweet smoked paprika

200g cooked quinoa or brown rice

2 tbsp good-quality balsamic vinegar

1 tsp Dijon mustard

1 tsp maple syrup

80g rocket leaves

400g tin of cannellini beans, drained and rinsed

10 radishes, very thinly sliced

1 medium fennel bulb, trimmed and very thinly sliced or shredded

40g pumpkin seeds

Sea salt and freshly ground black pepper, to taste

Put 2 tablespoons of the olive oil in a large pan and place over a medium heat. Add the garlic, cumin and paprika and cook gently for 2 minutes until aromatic. Add the cooked quinoa or rice and toss to combine. Season to taste and transfer to a large mixing or salad bowl.

To make the dressing, put the remaining olive oil into a small bowl or cup and add the balsamic vinegar, Dijon mustard and maple syrup. Whisk until everything comes together into a smooth dressing, then season to taste.

Add the rocket, beans, radishes, fennel, pumpkin seeds and dressing to the bowl of grains and gently toss to combine. Serve immediately.

NEW POTATO SALAD

Linda brought her potato salad alive with the flavours of fresh dill and finely chopped gherkins – it's a salad for all seasons. Just scrub the potatoes, as you lose valuable vitamin content if you peel them.

SERVES 4–6
AS A SIDE DISH

900g new potatoes,
    scrubbed clean
    and halved

140g vegan mayonnaise

1 tsp Dijon mustard

1 celery stick, tough
    strings removed,
    very finely chopped

60g pickled gherkins,
    very finely chopped

1½ tbsp lemon juice

2 tbsp chopped flatleaf
    parsley leaves

2 tbsp roughly chopped dill

Sea salt and freshly ground
    black pepper, to taste

Put the potatoes in a pan, cover with water and bring to the boil. Simmer gently until just tender, then drain well and leave to cool.

Transfer the potatoes to a large bowl and add the mayonnaise, mustard, celery, gherkins and lemon juice. Mix well and season generously, to taste. Stir through the parsley and dill just before serving.

QUINOA TABBOULEH SALAD

Using quinoa instead of the more traditional bulgur wheat makes this delicious version of tabbouleh a little different and gluten-free, plus quinoa is a good source of protein. The herbs are very finely chopped to marry with the other ingredients and the salad should look beautifully green.

SERVES 4–6

100g quinoa

2 large ripe tomatoes, finely diced

1 medium cucumber, finely diced

4 spring onions, trimmed

70g flatleaf parsley

40g mint, leaves only

2½ tbsp lemon juice

80ml extra virgin olive oil

1 medium garlic clove, peeled and crushed

Large pinch of ground allspice (optional)

25g pine nuts

Sea salt and freshly ground black pepper, to taste

Cook the quinoa according to the packet instructions, until tender, then leave to cool.

Meanwhile, put the diced tomatoes and cucumber into a bowl with half a teaspoon of salt and combine. Set aside for 15 minutes.

Put the spring onions, parsley (including the stems) and mint leaves into a food processor and pulse on and off until finely chopped. Alternatively, finely chop by hand.

Transfer the chopped herbs to a large mixing bowl. Tip the cucumber and tomato into a colander and drain off any liquid. Add them to the herbs, together with all the remaining ingredients, cooled quinoa and half a teaspoon of salt. Stir to combine and season to taste with more lemon juice and salt if necessary.

Serve immediately or leave for up to 30 minutes to let the flavours get to know one another.

"

WE ADMIRE BEAUTIFUL
BIRDS AND THEIR WINGS
AND FEATHERS AND
YET I WAS AT A DINNER
PARTY THE OTHER NIGHT
WHEN THEY WERE
PASSING AROUND BITS
OF CHICKEN AND I HEARD
SOMEBODY SAY 'I'LL HAVE
A WING, I'LL HAVE A LEG'.

"

Linda McCartney – 1995

BRIGHT MOROCCAN CARROT SALAD

Carrots are a great source of vitamins C and E as well as beta carotene, which the body converts to vitamin A, and may help to protect us against heart disease and cancer as well as eye conditions, such as cataracts. The orange in this salad makes it sweet and zingy – a real flavour sensation.

SERVES 4–6

1 orange

6 medium carrots
(about 450g), peeled
and coarsely grated

2 spring onions,
finely sliced

30g walnuts, finely chopped

½–1 tsp dried chilli flakes,
to taste

3 tbsp extra virgin olive oil

Juice of ½ lemon

Small handful of flatleaf
parsley, leaves only,
roughly chopped

Sea salt and freshly ground
black pepper, to taste

Start by segmenting the orange. A serrated knife is useful for this. First, cut off the top and bottom ends of the orange so you can set it flat on your chopping board. Working from top to bottom, slice away the peel and white pith, following the curve of the fruit. Insert the knife between one of the segments and its connective membrane and gently slice into the middle of the fruit. Then slice into the other side of the segment to release it from the membrane and lift it out. Repeat with the remaining segments.

Put the segments in a bowl with all the remaining ingredients and gently toss together. Season generously to taste. Cover and refrigerate the salad for about 30 minutes before serving.

SPINACH, AVOCADO AND MUSHROOM SALAD

Warm garlic mushrooms in this salad provide an earthy depth of flavour that goes perfectly with the creaminess of the ripe avocado. The three main ingredients here are rich in vitamins, and mushrooms are one of the few non-animal sources of vitamin D.

SERVES 4

70ml extra virgin olive oil

250g mushrooms, such as button, shiitake or portobello, wiped and thinly sliced

2 medium garlic cloves, peeled and crushed

6 spring onions, very thinly sliced

125g baby spinach leaves, washed and chopped

100g Little Gem lettuce leaves, roughly chopped

1½ tbsp good-quality balsamic vinegar

Squeeze of lemon juice

2 ripe avocados, peeled and stones removed (see p.23)

4 tbsp cooked vegan bacon bits (optional)

Sea salt and freshly ground black pepper, to taste

Put 3 tablespoons of the olive oil into a large frying pan and place over a medium-high heat. Add the mushrooms and fry, stirring now and again, for 8 minutes, until all the cooking juices have evaporated away and the mushrooms are golden and a little crispy around the edges. Add the garlic and fry for another 2 minutes until aromatic.

Put the spring onions, spinach, lettuce, vinegar, lemon juice and the rest of the olive oil into a large bowl, then gently mix together. Cut the avocado flesh into bite-sized pieces and add to the bowl, then sprinkle the mushrooms and bacon bits, if using, on top.

Season well to taste and serve immediately.

PANZANELLA SALAD

Part of helping to look after our planet is avoiding waste – particularly food waste. This salad, an Italian favourite, is the perfect way to use up bread that's a few days old. Stale bread is actually better than fresh here, as it holds its shape well and soaks up the flavour of the dressing.

SERVES 2

450g ripe mixed tomatoes, such as plum, cherry or heritage

½ small red onion, thinly sliced

1 medium garlic clove, peeled and crushed

1 tbsp capers, rinsed

2 tbsp red wine vinegar

2 tbsp extra virgin olive oil

2 thick slices of slightly stale sourdough bread

Handful of basil leaves, roughly torn

Sea salt and freshly ground black pepper, to taste

Cut the tomatoes into bite-sized wedges or chunks, making sure to save all the juices. Put them in a bowl or on a serving platter with the onion, garlic, capers, red wine vinegar and olive oil, then season generously to taste with salt and pepper.

Tear or cut the bread into small pieces, then add them to the salad with most of the basil, and gently mix together. Taste and adjust the seasoning with a little more oil, vinegar, salt or pepper if necessary.

Scatter over the remaining basil leaves and serve immediately.

PREP
15

COOK
5

GRANOLA BARS

These little bars of goodness will really keep you going, so they're ideal for breakfast or an afternoon snack on the go. The oats and rice provide carbohydrates and fibre, while the seeds are powerhouses of nutrients and contain essential fats. Dried apricots are a good source of iron. Wrap these up and off you go.

MAKES 12 BARS

110g oats (ordinary or
    gluten-free)
40g puffed rice
30g sunflower seeds
30g pumpkin seeds
60g unsulphured dried
    apricots, chopped
1 tsp ground cinnamon
¼ tsp sea salt
80g peanut butter
110ml maple syrup
50g coconut oil

Line a 26 x 22cm brownie tin with baking paper. Put the oats, puffed rice, sunflower and pumpkin seeds, dried apricots, cinnamon and salt into a bowl and mix together well.

Put the peanut butter, maple syrup and coconut oil into a pan and place over a medium heat. Stir constantly until the oil has melted and the mixture has come together. Take the pan off the heat and add the dry ingredients. Stir very thoroughly, so the oats and seeds are completely coated in the wet mixture and there are no clumps.

Spread the mixture out in the lined tin and press firmly into place with the back of a spoon. Leave to cool, then cover and refrigerate for at least 3 hours, or until completely set.

When ready to eat, slice into bars and gently remove from the tray. Serve immediately, or store in an airtight container for up to a week.

SESAME TOFU NOODLES

Tofu marinates really well, as it soaks up other flavours, such as soy, garlic and ginger, plus it's a good source of plant protein. This combo of noodles and tofu makes a perfect quick lunch or can be prepared the night before and packed into a container to enjoy on the go.

SERVES 4

3 tbsp toasted sesame oil

2 garlic cloves, peeled
   and crushed

2cm piece of fresh root
   ginger, peeled and
   finely grated

4 tbsp soy sauce or tamari

1 tsp maple syrup

2 tbsp crunchy
   peanut butter

3 tbsp rice vinegar

1–2 tbsp sriracha chilli
   sauce, to taste (optional)

300g soba buckwheat
   noodles

300g marinated tofu,
   cut into 1cm cubes

60g frozen edamame
   beans, defrosted

Large handful of coriander,
   finely chopped

4 spring onions,
   finely chopped

Put the sesame oil, garlic, ginger, soy sauce or tamari, maple syrup, peanut butter and rice vinegar into a large bowl with 2 tablespoons of water and whisk together until smooth. Add the sriracha to taste, if using, adding in more if you like your food very spicy. Cover and refrigerate until needed.

Cook the soba noodles according to the packet instructions in a pan of boiling water until just tender, taking care not to overcook them. Drain the noodles and immediately transfer them to a large bowl of cold water. Rinse them further under running cold water to remove the starchy coating. Drain thoroughly.

Remove the sauce from the fridge, add the cold drained noodles, tofu, edamame beans and most of the chopped coriander and spring onions and toss well to combine.

Transfer to bowls or lunchbox containers, scatter over the remaining coriander and spring onions, then cover and refrigerate until needed.

"

I'M OBSESSED WITH NATURE AND ANIMALS AND THE EARTH; I FIND CONCRETE THINGS DISTRACT ME.

"

Linda McCartney — 1989

BLACK-EYED BEAN CAKES

This is a wonderfully versatile recipe – you can experiment using other beans of your choice, such as kidney beans or black beans. Perfect served with a selection of dips or a leafy green salad.

SERVES 2–3
(MAKES 9 MINI CAKES)

2 tbsp milled flax seeds

400g tin of black-eyed beans, drained and rinsed

1 medium onion, peeled and roughly chopped

2 tbsp chopped parsley

¾ tsp each of allspice, ground cumin and sweet smoked paprika

2 tbsp ground almonds

30g white spelt or plain flour (or buckwheat for gluten-free)

3 tbsp sesame seeds

Extra virgin olive oil, to fry, plus extra to drizzle

Sea salt and freshly ground black pepper, to taste

To serve

80g rocket

100g hummus

2 tsp harissa

Put the flax seeds, beans, onion, parsley, spices, ground almonds, half a teaspoon of salt and quarter of a teaspoon of pepper into a food processor and blitz until smooth. Taste and, if you think it necessary, add more seasoning.

Put the flour in a bowl and the sesame seeds in another bowl. Scoop a heaped tablespoon – about 40g – of the mixture into the bowl of flour and toss gently to coat. Shake off any excess, then place the cake into the bowl of sesame seeds and gently press the seeds into the surface. Gently shape into a small burger patty and set aside. Continue with the remaining mixture.

Cover the base of a non-stick frying pan with a thin layer of olive oil. Place over a medium heat and, once hot, add the bean cakes, taking care not to overcrowd the pan. Fry the bean cakes in batches for 3–4 minutes on each side, until golden and crisp. Drain on kitchen paper while you fry the rest.

Serve immediately or pack the bean cakes into a lunchbox on a bed of rocket with some hummus and harissa.

PREP 10 **COOK 15**

PEA AND SPINACH PASTA

Quick and easy, this vibrant green pasta dish is packed with nutrition. It tastes great hot but is equally delicious at room temperature as a pasta salad, so makes an ideal lunchbox meal.

SERVES 2

60g fresh or frozen peas

190g bow or fusilli pasta, or another pasta of your choice

100g baby leaf spinach, washed

2 tbsp fresh oregano leaves

2 tbsp nutritional yeast flakes

2 tsp soy sauce or tamari

1 medium garlic clove, peeled and crushed

100ml dairy-free cream or plain yoghurt

1 tsp dried chilli flakes (optional)

Sea salt and freshly ground black pepper, to taste

Cook the peas in a large pan of boiling salted water for 3–4 minutes until tender. With a slotted spoon, transfer the peas to a bowl and leave the water on the boil. Add the pasta and cook according to the packet instructions.

Meanwhile, put the peas and the remaining ingredients, except the dried chilli flakes, into a food processor and blitz until smooth. Season to taste.

Drain the pasta, but reserve a little of the cooking water. Return the pasta to the hot dry pan and stir in the pea and spinach mixture and enough of the reserved pasta water to create a thick, creamy sauce. Taste and adjust the seasoning if necessary. Scatter over the chilli flakes, if using, before serving or piling into lunchboxes.

If making this the night before for a meal on the go, leave the lids off the lunchboxes until the pasta has cooled, then cover and refrigerate, ready to take with you the next morning.

QUICK
AND EASY
MEALS

HERBY MUSHROOM RISOTTO

Risotto is an Italian favourite made by stirring vegetable stock into rice to create a lovely creamy consistency. You can experiment with different varieties of mushrooms to find the flavour and texture you like best. Stir in the fresh herbs to complete the dish.

SERVES 4

6 tbsp extra virgin olive oil, plus extra to drizzle

500g mixed mushrooms, such as shiitake, chestnut, portobello or button, thinly sliced

2 medium garlic cloves, peeled and crushed

Handful of flatleaf parsley, leaves finely chopped

A few sprigs of tarragon, leaves finely chopped (optional)

2 medium onions, peeled and very finely chopped

800ml vegetable stock

175g risotto rice, such as arborio or carnaroli

50ml white wine or extra stock

35g non-dairy parmesan, finely grated (optional)

Salt and freshly ground black pepper, to taste

Preheat the oven to 200°C/Fan 180°C/Gas 6. Put 3 tablespoons of the oil into a large non-stick frying pan and place over a high heat. Add the mushrooms and sauté for 6–8 minutes, stirring regularly, until they release their juices and begin to soften. Add the garlic and fry for another 2 minutes until aromatic. Stir in most of the parsley and the tarragon, if using, and season to taste with salt and pepper. Transfer everything to a bowl, cover and set aside.

Put the pan back on the heat and add the remaining oil and the onions. Sauté for 8–10 minutes until the onions have softened but not coloured. Meanwhile, pour the vegetable stock into a separate pan and bring to a simmer.

Add the rice to the softened onions and stir until coated in the oil. Cook for a few minutes, then pour in the wine or extra stock. Keep stirring for a couple of minutes until the liquid has evaporated.

Add the vegetable stock from the pan a ladleful at a time, stirring until all the liquid has been absorbed before adding more stock. Continue like this until all but a ladleful of stock has been absorbed and the risotto is creamy. Stir in the mushrooms and their cooking juices and most of the non-dairy parmesan. Turn off the heat, put the lid on the pan and leave for 5 minutes to rest. If you prefer your risotto a little creamier, add a little more of the remaining stock.

Scatter over the rest of the non-dairy cheese and the parsley, then drizzle a little more olive oil over each serving.

ASPARAGUS, PEA AND RED PEPPER TART

Ready-rolled puff pastry is a great shortcut for vegans, as many shop-bought brands use vegetable shortening – but do always check the ingredients before buying. With the vibrant colours of the asparagus, sweet green peas and roasted red peppers, this tart looks as good as it tastes and is a perfect summer meal.

SERVES 4–6

320g ready-rolled sheet of vegan puff pastry

2 tbsp unsweetened plant-based milk of your choice, to glaze

200g asparagus, woody ends removed

100g frozen peas

150g vegan pesto, plus extra for drizzling

2 medium garlic cloves, peeled and crushed

200g roasted red peppers, from a jar, cut into strips

Sea salt and freshly ground black pepper, to taste

Preheat the oven to 200°C/Fan 180°C/Gas 6 and line a large baking sheet with baking paper. Unroll the pastry and place it on the lined baking sheet, then use a rolling pin to roll it out a little wider on the long side. Score a border about 2cm in from the edge, taking care not to cut all the way through. Prick the central area with a fork and brush the border with a little of the milk. Bake in the preheated oven for 15 minutes, until golden and almost cooked.

In the meantime, bring a large pan of salted water to the boil. Add the asparagus and peas, bring back to a rolling simmer and cook for 1–2 minutes, until barely cooked and still firm. Drain and refresh in cold water, then drain again. Transfer the vegetables to a clean tea towel and gently press out any excess water.

Remove the pastry from the oven and flatten the central area with the back of a spoon. Mix the vegan pesto with the garlic and spread the mixture over the tart, then layer the asparagus, peas and red pepper on top. Return to the oven and bake for another 10–15 minutes, until the tart is crisp and golden. Drizzle some extra pesto on top before serving.

Season generously with salt and pepper and serve immediately.

BLACK BEAN TACOS

Linda's cooking was influenced by her love of Mexican food and these tacos make a great Mexican-style feast. Choosing plant-based food is a compassionate step that helps prevent cruelty and suffering in animals, so go for pulses, such as black beans, as a way of filling your protein needs. Great served with guacamole – see the recipe on page 86.

SERVES 4

2 tbsp extra virgin olive oil, plus extra to drizzle

1 medium onion, peeled and finely chopped

5 medium garlic cloves, peeled and crushed

2 tsp ground cumin

1 tbsp sweet smoked paprika

2 x 400g tins of black beans, drained

200g ripe medium tomatoes, chopped

Sea salt and freshly ground black pepper, to taste

To serve

8 taco shells or tortillas

150g guacamole

150g salsa, from a jar

Large handful of fresh coriander, leaves only

1 tsp dried chilli flakes

Lime wedges

Heat the oil in a pan over a medium heat. Add the onion and garlic and cook gently for 8 minutes until softened, taking care not to let them burn.

Add the spices and cook for another 3 minutes until aromatic, then add the black beans, tomatoes and 250ml of water and bring to the boil. Reduce the heat and simmer for about 20 minutes or until almost all of the water has evaporated. Season with salt and pepper to taste.

Heat the tacos or tortillas. Serve the black beans on top with the guacamole and salsa, then sprinkle with fresh coriander leaves, chilli flakes and lime wedges.

CAPONATA

Aubergines have a satisfyingly meaty texture that works well in this version of the Sicilian classic. They're good for you too – rich in B vitamins and minerals. You can serve this on slices of toasted sourdough drizzled with oil, as a side dish, or stirred into a bowl of pasta.

SERVES 2–4

3 tbsp extra virgin olive oil

1 small onion, peeled and finely chopped

1 celery stick, strings removed, finely chopped

1 large aubergine, trimmed and cut into bite-sized pieces

30g black olives, pitted and roughly chopped

30g capers, rinsed

2 tbsp finely chopped flatleaf parsley leaves

1 tbsp red wine vinegar, plus extra to taste

2 tsp unrefined or caster sugar

200g tinned chopped tomatoes

1 tbsp tomato purée

Sea salt and freshly ground black pepper

To serve
Toasted sourdough

Put half the olive oil into a large pan with a lid and place over a medium-high heat. Add the onion and celery and cook gently for 5 minutes until they begin to soften. Put the remaining oil in a separate large frying pan and place over a medium-high heat. Add the aubergine and cook gently for 10 minutes until golden.

Transfer the aubergine to the pan of onion and celery, add the remaining ingredients and season to taste with salt and pepper. Cover the pan with a lid and simmer over a low heat for 30 minutes until everything is completely tender and soft.

Remove from the heat, allow to cool and leave to stand for at least 30 minutes at room temperature to allow the flavours to develop. Taste and adjust the seasoning with a little more salt and vinegar, if necessary. Serve at room temperature with some toasted sourdough, if you like.

*M*um's American background definitely influenced the food we ate at home. When I was growing up on our farm in East Sussex, things like macaroni cheese did not exist in the local village. You couldn't buy fancy ice cream, for instance, or bagels, pickles or mayonnaise, but all these things were common in our household.

Mexican food wasn't a big thing in England at that time, but because Mum had gone to the University of Arizona it was something she was familiar with. We all grew up loving Mexican food and other dishes from around the world. I think that Mum really loved being on the road with the band and every time she travelled to a new city or a new country, she would absorb the food culture, the ingredients and the menus and bring a little piece of that home to us.

PREP
15

COOK
20

BAKED LEEKS WITH BUTTER BEANS, GARLIC MAYO AND SOURDOUGH

This satisfying combo of creamy butter beans, sweet leeks and crunchy sourdough makes an excellent starter or an easy light meal that's tasty and nutritious.

SERVES 4

4 medium leeks
  (2 per person)

2 tbsp olive oil, plus
  extra to drizzle

400g tin of butter beans,
  drained and rinsed

Sea salt and freshly ground
  black pepper, to taste

To serve

4 tbsp vegan mayonnaise

1 small garlic clove, peeled
  and crushed

4 slices of sourdough bread

Flatleaf parsley

Preheat the oven to 200°C/Fan 180°C/Gas 6 and bring a large pan of salted water to the boil.

Trim the leeks, but make sure you don't take too much off the top, or they will fall apart when sliced. Cut the leeks in half lengthways and rinse under running water to remove any soil. Add them to the boiling water and cook for 3–4 minutes, until tender. Remove from the water and drain well.

Put the drained leeks in a roasting tray and add the 2 tablespoons of olive oil, then season well and bake for 10 minutes. Add the butter beans and bake for another 5 minutes until the leeks are slightly charred and crispy on the outside and tender on the inside.

Meanwhile, put the mayonnaise and garlic into a bowl and mix together. Toast the sourdough, drizzle with a little olive oil and season with a little salt and pepper.

Arrange the leeks and butter beans on top of the toasted sourdough, dollop over the garlic mayonnaise and scatter with some parsley. Serve immediately.

PREP 15   COOK 15

CRISPY GARLIC TOFU WITH PAK CHOI AND PEANUTS

This quick and easy dish has a great mix of textures and tastes, the crispy tofu contrasting beautifully with the tender greens, and the chilli, sesame oil and soy sauce bringing lots of vibrant flavour.

SERVES 2

280g block of firm tofu

2 tsp garlic powder

3 tbsp cornflour

5 tbsp vegetable oil

4 pak choi, trimmed and stalks separated

2 tsp roasted sesame oil

2 tsp soy sauce or tamari

4 tbsp roasted salted peanuts

1 red chilli, deseeded and thinly sliced (optional)

Sea salt and freshly ground black pepper

To serve

Cooked brown rice or noodles

Sriracha sauce (optional)

Squeeze of lime juice (optional)

Drain the tofu and wrap it in a clean tea towel. Place a heavy chopping board on top of the tofu and set it aside for 5 minutes.

Cut the block of tofu in half, and then each half into 1cm-thick slices. Season each slice of tofu with garlic powder and salt and pepper on both sides. Put the cornflour in a wide shallow bowl and add the slices of tofu in batches, turning them over a few times until they are evenly coated.

Put half the oil into a large non-stick pan and place over a medium-high heat. Add the tofu and fry for 2–3 minutes on each side until deeply golden and crispy, using more oil as necessary. Do this in batches so you don't overcrowd the pan. Remove each batch when it is ready and keep it warm in a low oven.

Add a little more oil to the pan and turn the heat up to high. Once hot, add the pak choi and 2 tablespoons of water and stir-fry for 2–3 minutes until vibrant green and tender. Remove from the heat and toss with the sesame oil and soy sauce.

Serve the crispy tofu and pak choi with the peanuts and chilli, if using, scattered over and some rice or noodles on the side. Add some sriracha chilli sauce and a squeeze of lime juice, if you like.

PAD THAI

This dish has become a takeaway and ready-meal favourite, but it is easy to make your own – then you know exactly what you're eating. Once you've prepared all the vegetables, this is ready to eat in 20 minutes. Tamarind paste is available in jars.

SERVES 2

2½ tbsp soy sauce or tamari

2½ tbsp unrefined or
    light brown sugar

2 tbsp tamarind paste
    mixed with 1 tbsp water,
    or 3 tbsp lime juice

200g flat rice noodles

Vegetable oil, to fry

150g broccoli florets,
    cut into small pieces

3 medium garlic cloves,
    peeled and crushed

100g bean sprouts

1 red chilli, deseeded
    and thinly sliced

3 spring onions,
    thinly sliced

50g roasted cashew
    nuts, roughly chopped

To serve

Handful of coriander leaves

Lime wedges

Put the soy sauce, sugar and the tamarind mixture or lime juice in a small saucepan and place over a medium heat. Warm through until the sugar dissolves completely, then remove from the heat.

Soak the noodles in hot water for 5–7 minutes until tender, but not completely soft.

Put 2 tablespoons of vegetable oil into a large frying pan and place over a high heat. Add the broccoli, garlic, bean sprouts and most of the chilli and spring onions – set some aside for later. Stir-fry for 2 minutes until the garlic is aromatic, taking care not to let it burn.

Drain the noodles and add them to the pan with the chopped cashew nuts, tossing them with the vegetables and separating any noodles that are sticking together. Add the soy sauce mixture and cook for another 3–5 minutes, tossing occasionally, until the noodles have soaked up most of the liquid and are tender. Taste and, if necessary, adjust the seasoning with more tamarind or soy sauce.

Plate up the noodles with the remaining spring onions and chilli scattered over the top and garnish with coriander leaves. Serve immediately with lime wedges on the side.

GREEN BEAN AND TOFU RED CURRY

Tofu is just right for curry recipes, as it soaks up all the spicy flavours so beautifully. This is a Thai-style curry and not too hot, but you can add more chilli if you like your food spicier. It's easy to prepare and makes a perfect warming mid-week supper. Curry paste is available in many food shops.

SERVES 4

1 tbsp coconut oil

3 tbsp red curry paste

400ml tin of coconut milk

400g tin of chopped tomatoes

2 lime leaves

400g firm tofu, drained and cut into 1cm cubes

300g green beans, trimmed

1 tsp coconut sugar or brown sugar

2½ tbsp soy sauce or tamari

Small handful of Thai basil, leaves only

1 red chilli, halved lengthways, deseeded and thinly sliced

2 tsp lime juice

To serve
Cooked rice
Lime wedges

Put the coconut oil and curry paste into a large pan and place over a high heat. Cook for 1–2 minutes until fragrant, then add the coconut milk, chopped tomatoes, lime leaves and tofu. Bring to the boil, then reduce the heat and simmer for 10 minutes until slightly thickened.

Add the green beans, sugar, soy sauce and most of the Thai basil and chilli – set some aside for later. Simmer for another 5 minutes until the green beans are just cooked through, with a little bite remaining. Stir in the lime juice, then taste to check the seasoning. Add a little more soy sauce or lime juice if required.

Serve in bowls with cooked rice, the remaining Thai basil and chilli scattered over the top and lime wedges on the side.

I HAVE A PASSION FOR PEACE AND I BELIEVE IT STARTS WITH COMPASSION FOR ANIMALS.

Linda McCartney – 1995

PREP
15

COOK
15

LEMON RICE WITH AUBERGINE, YOGHURT AND HERBS

This is a beautifully balanced quick-to-make meal with ingredients influenced by the colours and flavours of Middle Eastern food. Fragrant and delicious, it's naturally gluten-free too.

SERVES 2
OR 4 AS A SIDE

Small handful of finely chopped parsley leaves

2 tbsp finely chopped chives

½ small red onion, very finely sliced

340g cooked basmati or jasmine rice

Zest of 1 lemon and 2 tbsp juice

Extra virgin olive oil

1 aubergine, cut into 1cm-thick slices

¾ tsp sweet smoked paprika or ground cumin

Sea salt and freshly ground black pepper, to taste

To serve

100g unsweetened non-dairy coconut yoghurt

2 tbsp tahini

1 tbsp lemon juice

For the rice, put most of the parsley and chives into a bowl with the onion, cooked rice, lemon zest and juice and 4 tablespoons of olive oil. Season to taste and mix until combined, then set aside.

Meanwhile, put a couple of tablespoons of olive oil into a large pan and place over a medium-high heat. Working in batches, add the slices of aubergine and fry them for 5–7 minutes on each side until deeply golden. Add more oil as needed. Remove each batch, set aside and season to taste with smoked paprika or cumin and salt.

Mix the yoghurt with the tahini and lemon juice, then season with salt and pepper.

Serve the rice with the aubergine and scatter over the remaining parsley and chives. Season with a little more black pepper and serve with the yoghurt mixture on the side.

ROASTED SQUASH WITH PUY LENTILS AND ROCKET

Puy lentils work perfectly here, as they hold their shape well when cooked and their firm texture goes beautifully with the melting softness of the roast squash. If you're short of time you can use ready-cooked lentils, available in tins or pouches.

SERVES 4

1 medium butternut
   squash, halved
   lengthways and deseeded

3 tbsp olive oil

300g Puy lentils,
   washed and drained

3 garlic cloves, peeled
   and crushed

1 litre vegetable stock

2 tbsp red wine vinegar

2 tbsp soy sauce or tamari

100g rocket

Sea salt and freshly ground
   black pepper, to taste

To serve

Zest of 1 lemon

4 tbsp non-dairy crème
   fraîche or yoghurt

60g roasted walnuts

Small handful of flatleaf
   parsley, leaves only

Preheat the oven to 220°C/Fan 200°C/Gas 7. Cut the squash into 2cm wedges and put them in a roasting tin. Coat with a tablespoon of the oil and season generously, then roast for 20–25 minutes until tender and golden.

Meanwhile, put the lentils, garlic and vegetable stock into a large saucepan and bring to the boil. Reduce the heat to a simmer, cover and cook for about 20–25 minutes or until the lentils are tender, but still with a little bite, and most of the stock has been absorbed. Pour off any excess stock, then add the vinegar, soy sauce and the remaining oil and stir to combine. Season to taste.

When ready to serve, fold the rocket through the lentils and divide between 4 plates. Place the wedges of roasted squash on top. Stir the lemon zest through the crème fraîche or yoghurt and dollop on top, then scatter over the walnuts and parsley. Season with a little more salt and pepper and serve immediately.

PREP
10
COOK
15

KIMCHI PANCAKES

A staple in Korea, kimchi or fermented cabbage is full of flavour and super nutritious. It's widely available in supermarkets and health food stores now. This recipe makes two quite hearty pancakes, which provide a full meal for two people or a starter for four. If you fancy a bit more heat, add some chilli oil to the dipping sauce.

SERVES 2–4

260g kimchi, roughly
   chopped

140g white spelt or
   plain flour

2 tbsp cornflour

90ml kimchi liquid,
   strained from a jar
   or bag of kimchi

2 medium garlic cloves,
   peeled and crushed

½ tsp coconut palm
   or brown sugar

Large pinch of sea salt

Vegetable oil, to fry

Dipping sauce

3 tbsp soy sauce or tamari

1 tbsp rice wine vinegar
   or chilli oil (optional)

To serve

2 spring onions,
   very thinly sliced

Put the kimchi into a bowl with both flours, the kimchi liquid, garlic, sugar, salt and 120ml of water and mix to form a thick batter.

For the dipping sauce, put the soy sauce and rice wine vinegar or chilli oil, if using, into a small bowl. Stir and set aside.

Cover the base of a large non-stick frying pan with a thin layer of vegetable oil and set over a high heat. When hot, pour half the batter into the pan and spread it out into a flat round. Fry for 3–4 minutes on one side, until golden and crispy, then flip over and drizzle in another 1 or 2 teaspoons of vegetable oil around the edges of the pancake. Fry until golden and crispy, then slide on to a plate or board. Cook the remaining batter in the same way.

To serve, cut into wedges and scatter over the spring onions. Serve immediately with the dipping sauce.

PREP
15

COOK
20

THAI CORN FRITTERS

Linda was a big sweetcorn fan, enjoying it fresh off the cob in the height of summer. By using frozen or canned corn, you can make these flavour-packed fritters at any time of the year. Perfect for lunch with a crisp green salad or as a starter – or as a great addition to a weekend brunch. Whether fresh, frozen or canned, sweetcorn contains plenty of fibre and is rich in vitamins.

SERVES 4

400g frozen or tinned
  sweetcorn

1 tbsp milled flax seeds

3 tbsp hot water

110g white spelt flour

¼ tsp dried chilli flakes
  or 1 fresh red chilli,
  deseeded and chopped

1 tsp ground cumin

1 tsp ground coriander

1 small red onion, peeled
  and very finely chopped

2 medium garlic cloves,
  peeled and crushed

3 tbsp chopped fresh
  coriander

1 tbsp soy sauce or tamari

90ml unsweetened plant-
  based milk of your choice

Vegetable oil, to fry

To serve
Chopped coriander
Lime or lemon wedges
Sweet chilli sauce

Defrost the sweetcorn, if using frozen, or drain and rinse if using tinned. Put the flax seeds in a large mixing bowl with the hot water, stir and set aside for 5 minutes. Add all the remaining ingredients, except the oil, and mix well.

Cover the base of a large non-stick frying pan with a thin layer of vegetable oil and place over a medium-high heat. Place heaped tablespoons of the batter into the pan and gently flatten into discs, taking care not to overcrowd the pan – you'll need to cook these fritters in batches. Fry for 3–5 minutes on each side until crisp and deeply golden brown. Transfer to a plate lined with kitchen paper, sprinkle with a little salt and keep them warm in a low oven while you fry the rest.

Serve immediately with a little more coriander scattered over the top, lime or lemon wedges and some sweet chilli sauce on the side.

BARBECUE SAUSAGE AND VEGETABLE SKEWERS

This combo of vegan sausages and juicy glazed vegetables is really delicious and popular with everyone, vegan or not. These are best cooked on the barbecue but are almost as good cooked indoors when the weather is bad.

SERVES 2
(MAKES 6 SKEWERS)

1 courgette, cut into
    1cm-thick slices

1 large red onion, peeled and
    cut into wedges

1 red pepper, deseeded and
    cut into bite-sized pieces

18 mushrooms, such as
    button or shiitake

6 Linda McCartney
    vegetarian sausages,
    or others of your choice,
    cut into chunks

3 tbsp olive oil

1 tbsp balsamic vinegar

3 tsp mustard

1 garlic clove, peeled
    and crushed

2 tbsp basil, finely chopped

Sea salt and freshly ground
    black pepper

Soak 6 wooden skewers in a bowl of water and set them aside until you are ready to use them.

To make the barbecue sauce, if using, mix all the ingredients in a bowl and set aside.

Put the vegetables, mushrooms and sausages into a bowl with the olive oil, vinegar, mustard, garlic and basil and season generously to taste. Gently mix together until evenly coated.

Thread the vegetables and sausages on to the soaked skewers, ensuring an even distribution of each.

Cook the skewers on a barbecue, griddle or in a frying pan for 8–10 minutes, turning them now and again until evenly charred on all sides and cooked through. Serve immediately with barbecue sauce, if you like.

Barbecue sauce (optional)

340ml tomato ketchup

85g brown sugar

140ml vinegar

Juice of 1/2 lemon

3 garlic cloves, peeled and
    crushed or 2 tsp garlic
    powder

2 tbsp green relish or
    chopped pickle

2 tbsp mild mustard

6 tbsp vegetable oil

Sea salt and freshly ground
    black pepper, to taste

CHINESE-STYLE FRIED RICE

This is a home-made version of a Chinese takeaway favourite. It's a great way of using up any leftover rice – we hate food waste – and it is easy to put together for a quick supper. Just make sure the leftover rice has been cooled quickly and stored in the fridge.

SERVES 4

3 tbsp vegetable oil

1 medium carrot, peeled
   and finely chopped

1 small onion, peeled
   and finely chopped

150g bean sprouts

3 medium garlic cloves,
   peeled and crushed

150g frozen peas, defrosted

800g cooked jasmine or
   basmati rice, preferably a
   day old and refrigerated

3 tbsp soy sauce or tamari

2 tsp roasted sesame oil

To serve

3 spring onions, very
   thinly sliced

Put the oil into a large pan and place over a medium heat. Add the carrot and sauté for 5 minutes until it begins to soften. Add the onion, bean sprouts, garlic and peas and sauté for another 5–6 minutes until softened.

Turn the heat up to high, add the rice, soy sauce and sesame oil and stir to combine. Fry for 6–8 minutes, until golden, piping hot and slightly crispy in places. Taste and adjust the seasoning with a little more soy sauce and sesame oil, if necessary.

Scatter the spring onions over the top and serve at once.

PREP 10 COOK 15

RICE NOODLES WITH EDAMAME BEANS, BROCCOLI, GINGER AND GARLIC

Edamame beans are young soya beans and are widely available fresh or frozen. They're low in calories but are a great source of protein, vitamins and minerals, so they make an excellent addition to this quick noodle stir-fry.

SERVES 4

200g rice vermicelli
  noodles

2 tbsp vegetable oil

1 tbsp roasted sesame oil

200g edamame beans or
  peas (frozen are fine)

1 medium carrot, peeled
  and cut into matchstick-
  sized strips

300g tenderstem broccoli

2 tbsp hot water

6cm piece of fresh root
  ginger, peeled and
  very finely chopped

2 garlic cloves, crushed

5 spring onions,
  finely sliced

2½ tbsp soy sauce or tamari

2 tsp sesame seeds

To serve

Lime wedges

Sriracha sauce (optional)

Fresh coriander

Cook the noodles according to the packet instructions, then rinse them in cold water, drain and set aside.

Meanwhile, put the vegetable oil and a teaspoon of the sesame oil in a pan and place over a medium-high heat. Once hot, add the edamame beans or peas, carrot, broccoli and 2 tablespoons of hot water, and fry for 5 minutes. Add the ginger and garlic and fry for another 2 minutes, then add half of the spring onions and fry for a final minute.

Add the cooked noodles, soy sauce, most of the sesame seeds and the remaining roasted sesame oil. Toss everything together until the noodles are hot. Taste and adjust the seasoning with a little more soy sauce or sesame oil if necessary, then sprinkle over the remaining spring onions and sesame seeds. Serve with a squeeze of lemon and sriracha sauce, if using, and fresh coriander leaves.

MEDITERRANEAN CHICKPEA PANCAKES

These come with a warning – they are addictive! Once you start eating them, it is hard to stop. We've suggested toppings below but once you've got the knack of these pancakes, experiment with your own ideas. Served with a green salad, they make a perfect quick meal. Chickpea or gram flour is available in most supermarkets now.

SERVES 4

200g chickpea (gram) flour
340ml sparkling water
4 tbsp extra virgin olive oil
½ tsp salt

To serve
Extra virgin olive oil
2 spring onions, very
     finely chopped
About 30 black and green
     olives, stones removed
     and roughly chopped
Large handful of flatleaf
     parsley leaves,
     roughly chopped
6 semi-dried tomatoes,
     drained and roughly
     chopped
Sea salt and freshly
     ground black pepper

Sieve the chickpea flour into a large bowl with half a teaspoon of salt. Slowly whisk in the sparkling water, making sure there are no lumps.

Add 2 tablespoons of olive oil to a large non-stick frying pan, ideally 22–24cm in diameter, and place over a high heat. When the oil is very hot, almost smoking, pour in half the batter, swirling the pan around so it is evenly distributed. Leave over the high heat for 2 minutes, then turn the heat down to medium and continue to cook for another 1–2 minutes until the base is golden and crispy and the surface has almost dried out. Flip the pancake over and fry for another minute until fully cooked, then slide it on to a plate. Add the remaining 2 tablespoons of oil and cook the rest of the batter in the same way.

To serve, drizzle over a generous amount of extra virgin olive oil, as this helps both the flavour and texture. Season with salt and black pepper, then divide the spring onions, olives, parsley and tomatoes between the 2 pancakes. Cut into wedges as a side dish or starter and serve immediately.

WEEKEND FEASTS

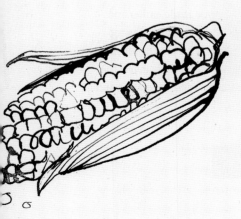

PREP 20 COOK 1h30

LASAGNE

The smell of Linda's lasagne cooking was so tempting and this treat was always devoured moments after being served. Here is a vegan version of her classic – layers of pasta smothered in her moreish vegan sauce.

SERVES 6

4 tbsp extra virgin olive oil

1 medium onion, peeled and chopped

1 celery stick, tough strings removed, finely chopped

2 garlic cloves, peeled and crushed

300g Linda McCartney vegan mince, or alternative of your choice

1 tbsp tomato purée

400g tin of tomatoes

2 tsp dried oregano

1 tbsp soy sauce or tamari

250ml vegetable stock

40g plain flour

500ml unsweetened plant-based milk of your choice (oat works well)

3 tbsp nutritional yeast

8–12 egg-free lasagne sheets

250g dairy-free cheese, grated

Sea salt and freshly ground black pepper, to taste

Preheat the oven to 180°C/Fan 160°C/Gas 4. Put 2 tablespoons of the oil into a large saucepan and place over a medium heat. Add the onion and celery and cook them gently for 10–15 minutes until softened. Add the garlic and cook for another minute until aromatic. Increase the heat, add the mince and fry for another 5 minutes, stirring now and again, until the mince has browned.

Stir in the tomato purée, chopped tomatoes, oregano, soy sauce and stock, then season to taste with salt and pepper. Bring to the boil, then reduce the heat and simmer, stirring now and again, for 20–30 minutes, until reduced. Taste and adjust the seasoning if necessary.

Meanwhile, put the remaining 2 tablespoons of oil into another pan and place over a medium heat. Once hot, add the flour and cook, stirring all the time, for 1 minute. Gradually add the milk, whisking constantly, until smooth. Add the nutritional yeast and simmer gently for 5 minutes, stirring all the time, until you have a thick white sauce. Season generously to taste with salt and pepper.

Check the instructions on your packet of lasagne sheets and, if necessary, soak them in water.

Spread a layer of the mince over the base of a medium-sized baking dish. Arrange some lasagne sheets on top, spoon a thin layer of white sauce over them, then scatter over some grated cheese. Repeat this process until you've used all your ingredients, finishing with a layer of white sauce and dairy-free cheese.

Bake in the oven for 30–35 minutes until the cheese is bubbling and golden and the pasta is cooked through.

SHEPHERD'S PIE

This book is jam-packed with our family favourites and shepherd's pie is one of our top loves. The Puy lentils hold their shape well when cooked and are combined with vegetables and vegan mince in a tasty gravy. Try adding a little mustard to the mash for an extra kick of flavour, if you like.

SERVES 6

1.2kg potatoes, peeled and quartered

100g non-dairy butter

200ml soya milk

2 tbsp extra virgin olive oil

1 medium onion, peeled and finely chopped

1 celery stick, tough strings removed, finely chopped

2 medium carrots, peeled and finely chopped

2 medium garlic cloves, peeled and crushed

350g Linda McCartney vegan mince, or alternative of your choice

200g tinned Puy lentils, drained

2 tbsp tomato purée

2 x 400g cans of chopped tomatoes

2 tbsp soy sauce or tamari

450ml vegetable stock

Sea salt and freshly ground black pepper, to taste

Preheat the oven to 200°C/Fan 180°C/Gas 6.

Put the potatoes in a pan of salted water and bring to the boil. Simmer for 15–20 minutes, until completely tender. Drain thoroughly, tip them back into the hot pan and leave to steam dry for 10 minutes. Mash with the butter and milk until smooth, then season generously to taste with salt and pepper and set aside.

Meanwhile, put the olive oil into a large saucepan and place over a medium heat. Add the onion, celery and carrots and sweat for 10–15 minutes until softened. Add the garlic and cook for another minute until aromatic. Increase the heat, add the mince and lentils, then fry for another 5 minutes, stirring now and again, until browned.

Stir in the tomato purée, chopped tomatoes, soy sauce, stock and season to taste. Bring to the boil, then reduce the heat and simmer, stirring now and again, for 20–30 minutes, until reduced. Taste and add more salt and pepper if necessary.

Transfer the mince mixture to a large casserole dish and cover with the mashed potato. Bake for 30 minutes until the mash is golden. Serve immediately.

MUSHROOM AND LENTIL PIE

There's something very comforting about a pie and this one, filled with a savoury mixture of mushrooms, herbs and lentils, is no exception. If you don't have a bottle of brandy to hand, no problem – leave it out or have a look for the miniatures you can buy. Ready-rolled pastry is a great time saver, but check the ingredients are suitable for vegans.

SERVES 6–8

500g ready-rolled vegan shortcrust pastry

4 tbsp extra virgin olive oil

1 medium onion, peeled and finely chopped

450g mixed mushrooms, thinly sliced

2 medium garlic cloves, peeled and crushed

2 tbsp white spelt or plain flour, plus extra to dust

330ml soya or oat cream

1 tbsp brandy (optional)

2 tbsp finely chopped fresh tarragon leaves

400g tin of Puy lentils, drained and rinsed

2 tbsp unsweetened plant-based milk of your choice, to seal

Sea salt and freshly ground black pepper, to taste

Preheat the oven to 200°C/Fan 180°C/Gas 6. Divide the pastry into 2 pieces, one slightly bigger than the other. Line a 20cm pie dish with the larger piece of pastry, letting it overhang the edges by about 2cm.

Put the oil in a large frying pan and place over a medium-high heat. Add the onion and sauté for 5 minutes until it begins to soften, then add the mushrooms and sauté for a further 10–12 minutes until the onion is fully softened and translucent and the mushrooms have released all their liquid and turned golden. Add the garlic and sauté for another 2 minutes until aromatic.

Move the onion and mushrooms to the side of the pan and add the flour to the centre. Cook over a medium heat for 2 minutes, stirring all the time, then combine the flour with the onion and mushrooms.

Slowly pour in the cream, a little at a time, stirring constantly until you have a smooth, lump-free sauce. Add the brandy, if using, the tarragon, lentils and 1½ teaspoons of salt and ½ teaspoon of pepper. Simmer for 5 minutes, then remove the pan from the heat. Taste and season with more salt and pepper, if necessary, and leave to cool.

Pour the mushroom and lentil mixture into the pastry-lined pie dish. Brush the border of the pastry with milk and top with the remaining piece of pastry. Crimp the sides to seal the pastry, cutting off any excess. Cut a cross, or any other design you like, in the centre to create a steam hole. Bake for 45–50 minutes until the pastry is a deep golden colour and crispy. Serve immediately.

AUBERGINE AND TOMATO BAKE

This really is a feast – layers of succulent aubergine and tangy Kalamata olive and tomato sauce, all topped with vegan mozzarella and crunchy pine nuts. Mouthwatering. Any leftovers keep well for a couple of days and can be reheated for a quick lunch.

SERVES 4

- 100ml olive oil, plus extra to grease
- 1 medium onion, peeled and finely chopped
- 2 garlic cloves, peeled and crushed
- 2 x 400g tins of chopped tomatoes
- 140g tomato purée
- 80g Kalamata olives, roughly chopped
- 2 tbsp roughly chopped fresh oregano leaves
- 2 tbsp roughly chopped fresh basil leaves
- 1 tbsp balsamic vinegar
- 60g plain or white spelt flour
- 2 aubergines, trimmed and cut lengthways into 5mm-thick slices
- 200g vegan mozzarella cheese, grated
- 2 tbsp pine nuts
- Sea salt and freshly ground black pepper

Preheat the oven to 180°C/Fan 160°C/Gas 4 and lightly grease a medium-sized baking dish with oil.

Put 2 tablespoons of the oil into a large pan with a lid and place over a medium-high heat. Add the onion and cook gently for 8–10 minutes until softened. Add the garlic, tomatoes, tomato purée, olives, herbs, vinegar, a teaspoon of salt and a quarter of a teaspoon of pepper, then bring to a gentle simmer. Cover with a lid and cook over a low heat for 30 minutes, stirring now and again, until slightly reduced. Taste and adjust the seasoning if necessary.

Meanwhile, place the flour in a wide shallow bowl and season generously with salt and pepper. Coat each slice of aubergine in the seasoned flour and set aside. Put another 2 tablespoons of the olive oil into a large non-stick frying pan and place over a medium-high heat. Working in batches, so as not to overcrowd the pan, fry the floured aubergine slices for 3–4 minutes on each side until golden. Continue until all are fried, adding more oil as needed.

Cover the base of the greased baking dish with a thin layer of the tomato sauce, then add a layer of aubergine and continue layering until you have used up all of the ingredients. Mix the grated mozzarella with the pine nuts and scatter over the top of the dish. Season with a little more salt and pepper and bake for 30–40 minutes until the top is golden brown and bubbling. Serve immediately.

Mum and Dad really started a revolution when they became vegetarian. They were so united on that journey and it meant so much to them. As a family, we always talked a lot about what to eat, and when we gave up meat, we really didn't miss it at all. Because Mum was such a great cook, she had a way of infusing everything she made with so much flavour. She just loved feeding people and seeing them enjoy her food.

Mum was a very gentle and kind person, but she didn't hesitate to speak up about what she believed in. She was feisty – in a good way. She always tried to engage people and to persuade them to stop eating meat. She would say that animals don't have a voice, so she was speaking on their behalf to try and save them. She was passionate about nature, animal rights and the environment, and we have all inherited her strong attitudes.

Mary

BAKED MACARONI CHEESE

When the family first gave up meat, Linda created a turkey-shaped macaroni cheese so there was something to carve at the Christmas lunch table! It's lovely with some salad or green vegetables at any time of year. The 'cheesy' taste comes from the nutritional yeast flakes – a natural product that can add extra flavour in many recipes.

SERVES 4

50g raw unsalted cashew
  nuts, finely chopped

¾ tsp turmeric powder

40g nutritional yeast

1½ tbsp miso

2 tsp apple cider vinegar

1 tsp fine sea salt

½ tsp onion powder

¾ tsp garlic powder

½ tsp sweet
  smoked paprika

1½ tbsp Dijon mustard

350g macaroni

30g fresh breadcrumbs

1 tbsp extra virgin olive oil,
  plus extra to grease

Sea salt

Put the chopped cashew nuts into a pan of boiling water and cook them for 10 minutes over a high heat. Drain them thoroughly in a fine sieve and transfer to a high-speed blender. Add the rest of the ingredients, except the macaroni, breadcrumbs and oil, and 230ml of water, then blitz until completely smooth. This may take a few minutes, depending on the power of your blender. Taste and adjust the seasoning if necessary.

Preheat the oven to 180°C/Fan 160°C/Gas 4. Grease a medium baking dish with a little olive oil.

Cook the macaroni in a pan of boiling, salted water for 1–2 minutes less than the packet instructions – the pasta should be still be quite al dente, not soft. Drain thoroughly and transfer to the baking dish. Add the sauce and stir to combine. Scatter over the breadcrumbs, drizzle over the olive oil and bake in the oven for 15 minutes until golden and crisp on top.

PREP
20

COOK
1h

DEEP DISH PIE

This is a totally gorgeous pie – bring this to the table and everyone will sigh with delight.
And as we use ready-made vegan pastry and burgers or meatballs, it is easy to put
together. The pastry is widely available but just check the ingredients label to make
sure it is vegan. A bowl of green peas is the perfect accompaniment.

SERVES 4–6

2 tbsp olive oil

1 large onion, peeled
and chopped

250g button mushrooms,
thinly sliced

3 garlic cloves, peeled
and finely chopped

1 tbsp white spelt or
plain flour

480g Linda McCartney
meatballs (or burgers),
roughly chopped, or
others of your choice

1 tsp fresh thyme,
leaves only

250ml vegetable stock

2 tsp wholegrain mustard

1 tbsp soy sauce or tamari

1 tbsp balsamic vinegar

320g vegan puff
pastry sheet

Plant-based milk of your
choice, to brush over

Sea salt and freshly ground
black pepper

Put the oil into a large non-stick frying pan and place over a medium-
high heat. Add the onion and mushrooms and sauté for 12–15
minutes until the mushroom juices have been released and have
evaporated, so the pan is mostly dry and the mushrooms are golden.
Add the garlic and cook for another 3 minutes until aromatic.

Mix in the flour and cook for 3 minutes, stirring frequently. Add the
vegetarian meatballs or burgers, thyme and stock and bring to the
boil. Reduce the heat and simmer for 5 minutes until the sauce is
thickened. Stir in the mustard, soy sauce and balsamic vinegar and
cook for another 3 minutes. Season to taste.

Preheat the oven to 220°C/Fan 200°C/Gas 7. Turn a 23cm pie dish
upside down and place it on top of the rolled-out sheet of puff pastry.
Cut around the perimeter of the dish, leaving an extra centimetre
of pastry overlapping. Turn the dish right side up and tip in the pie
mixture. Dampen the rim of the dish with a little water, then carefully
place the puff pastry lid on top and crimp the edges into place.

If you like, you can use the leftover pastry to create cut-outs for the
top of the pie – leaves, letters or whatever you like. Brush the pastry
gently with a little milk and make a hole in the centre of the pastry
for the steam to escape while the pie is cooking.

Bake the pie in the preheated oven for 10 minutes, then reduce the
heat to 200°C/Fan 180°C/Gas 6 and cook for another 15–20 minutes
until the pastry is deeply golden and crisp. Serve immediately.

"

THE GREATEST COOKS
I'VE EVER MET HAVE
ALL BEEN SELF-TAUGHT
PEOPLE WHO HAVE
DEVELOPED THEIR SKILLS
MAINLY THROUGH THEIR
LOVE OF GOOD FOOD.

"

Linda McCartney – 1989

PULLED JACKFRUIT BURGERS

It can take 2,350 litres of fresh water to produce just one 150g beef burger – that's enough water to fill 30 bathtubs or have a five-hour shower! So that's a good reason to try this sensational pulled pork-style jackfruit instead and enjoy the burger experience without harming the environment. You can buy jackfruit in jars and tins.

SERVES 4

2 x 400g tins or jars of jackfruit in water

2 tbsp olive oil

3 garlic cloves, crushed

2 tsp sweet smoked paprika

1½ tsp ground cumin

5 tbsp soy sauce or tamari

3 tbsp maple syrup

2 tbsp balsamic vinegar

3 tbsp tomato purée

Sea salt and freshly ground black pepper

To serve

8 cos lettuce leaves

4 burger buns

4 slices of vegan cheese (optional)

½ small red onion, peeled and finely sliced

1 large tomato, thinly sliced

Drain the jackfruit, rinse it thoroughly and pat dry. Cut it into thin slices.

Put the oil into a large non-stick pan and place over a high heat. Add the jackfruit and stir-fry for 5–7 minutes, until it begins to colour. Add the garlic, paprika and cumin and fry for another minute until aromatic. Reduce the heat to medium, add the soy sauce, maple syrup, vinegar and tomato purée and simmer for another 3–4 minutes, stirring frequently, until all the liquid has reduced down and the jackfruit has thickened and become sticky. Taste and adjust the seasoning if necessary with salt and pepper.

To serve, place some lettuce on the base of a burger bun, top with vegan cheese, if using, slices of red onion, tomato and the jackfruit. Place the other half of the bun on top and serve immediately.

PREP
30

COOK
40

PIZZA

Home-made pizzas are such fun to put together and you can go wild with your topping ideas – we've suggested a few below to get you started. Just make sure you allow time for your dough to rise, and get your pan and oven really, really hot for a crisp base.

SERVES 4

Dough

400g white spelt or
    plain flour, plus
    extra for dusting

100g wholegrain flour

2 x 7g sachets of
    instant yeast

2 tsp fine sea salt

2 tsp maple syrup

300ml warm water

Topping suggestions

Tomato passata or sauce
    (see p.198)

Non-dairy mozzarella

Griddled vegetables,
    such as courgettes,
    peppers (see p.196)

Roasted red peppers

Chargrilled artichokes

Olives, capers, sun-dried
    tomatoes

Pesto, herbs, rocket

Extra virgin olive oil,
    to drizzle

Put the flours, yeast and salt into the bowl of a stand mixer fitted with a dough hook and stir to combine. Add the maple syrup and water, switch on the machine and knead for 5 minutes until the dough comes together into a ball. Alternatively, knead the dough by hand for about 7–10 minutes until smooth and springy.

Place the dough in a bowl covered with oiled cling film. Leave to rise for 1–1½ hours or until at least doubled in size – the exact time will depend on the temperature of your kitchen. You can also leave the dough to rise overnight in the fridge.

Preheat your oven to the hottest setting, at least 240°C/Fan 220°C/Gas 9. Once the dough has doubled in size, knead it once or twice, make it into a ball, then divide the dough into 4 pieces of equal size.

When ready to cook, roll out a ball of dough into a thin round, dusting with a little flour now and again to prevent sticking. Place a large ovenproof pan over a very high heat. Once the pan is smoking hot, carefully place the round of dough on to the pan. Quickly add your toppings of choice and cook for 3–5 minutes until the base is crispy and slightly charred and the edges are puffing up.

Carefully transfer the pan to the hot oven and cook for another 3–5 minutes, depending on the heat of your oven, until cooked through and the toppings are melted and golden. Serve immediately while you cook the remaining pizzas.

VEGETABLE PAELLA

The chargrilled artichokes in jars are perfect for this paella and give it an authentic Spanish taste. A great one-pot supper that's bursting with colourful vegetables and rich flavours.

SERVES 4

2 tbsp olive oil

1 large onion, peeled
    and chopped

325g short-grain brown rice

4 garlic cloves, peeled and
    finely chopped

800ml vegetable stock

Large pinch of saffron
    threads, soaked in
    1 tbsp hot water

1 tsp sweet smoked paprika

¼ tsp ground turmeric

5 large tomatoes, roughly
    chopped, keeping all
    the juices

175g frozen peas

1 red pepper, deseeded
    and roughly chopped

180g green beans, trimmed

10 chargrilled artichoke
    quarters, from a jar

Sea salt and freshly ground
    black pepper, to taste

To serve

1 lemon, cut into wedges

Small handful of flatleaf
    parsley, leaves only

Put the oil in a large non-stick frying pan and place over a medium-high heat. Add the onion and cook gently for 8–10 minutes until it begins to soften. Add the rice and garlic and cook for 3 minutes until aromatic.

Add the stock, saffron, paprika, turmeric and the tomatoes and their juices, then bring to the boil. If the stock is not already salted, season to taste. Simmer for 25 minutes, then spread the remaining vegetables over the rice, pushing them down into the rice slightly with a spoon. Simmer for another 10–15 minutes until the rice and vegetables are cooked through and have absorbed all the stock. Taste and adjust the seasoning if necessary.

Serve with the lemon wedges and parsley scattered over the top.

HEARTY VEGETABLE STEW

Linda made the best vegetable stews, packed with flavour and so comforting. They always tasted so good and when she was asked for her secret, she would say that the celery and cabbage were essential ingredients and added that special something.

SERVES 4

1 red pepper, deseeded

4 medium carrots, peeled

4 medium potatoes, peeled

150g kale

3 tbsp extra virgin olive oil

1 medium onion, peeled and finely chopped

3 garlic cloves, peeled and crushed

1 tbsp fresh thyme or rosemary, leaves only

2 celery sticks, tough strings removed, cut into small dice

200g vegan meat pieces or smoked tofu, chopped

400g tin of chopped tomatoes

800ml vegetable stock

3 tbsp soy sauce or tamari

2 tbsp chopped parsley

Sea salt and freshly ground black pepper

Chop the red pepper, carrots, potatoes and kale into bite-sized pieces.

Put the oil in a pan and place over a medium-high heat. Add the onion and red pepper and cook gently for 10 minutes until softened. Add the garlic and thyme or rosemary, then fry for another 2 minutes until aromatic.

Add the carrots, potatoes, celery, vegan meat or tofu, tomatoes, stock and soy sauce and bring to the boil. Reduce the heat and season to taste with salt and pepper. Cover with a lid and simmer gently over a low heat for 25 minutes. Add the kale and continue to cook until all the vegetables are completely tender and the stock has thickened slightly.

Scatter over the parsley and serve immediately. Any leftovers can be kept in the fridge in an airtight container. In fact, the stew tastes even better the next day when the flavours intensify.

"HORSES, RHINOCEROS, BUFFALO, ELEPHANT ARE ALL VEGETARIANS AND YET THEY'RE OUR STRONGEST ANIMALS"

SIDES
AND
SNACKS

MEXICAN-STYLE SWEET POTATOES

Bursting with flavour, colour and nutrition, this sweet potato dish is really moreish. What's more, it's rich in protein, antioxidants and vitamins – and so easy to make.

SERVES 4

4 large sweet potatoes

2 tsp chipotle paste

3 tbsp extra virgin olive oil, plus extra to drizzle

1 onion, peeled and finely chopped

2cm piece of fresh root ginger, peeled and grated

3 garlic cloves, peeled and crushed

400g tin of refried beans

60ml vegetable stock

240g cherry tomatoes, halved

Sea salt and freshly ground black pepper, to taste

To serve

2 ripe avocados

½ tsp dried chilli flakes

Handful of coriander, leaves only

Preheat the oven to 220°C/Fan 200°C/Gas 7.

Cut the sweet potatoes in half lengthways. Mix the chipotle paste with half the olive oil and coat the cut sides of the potatoes. Season generously and place on a baking tray. Bake for 30–40 minutes, depending on the size of the potatoes, until the flesh is soft and buttery and the skin is crisp.

Meanwhile, heat the remaining oil in a pan over a medium heat. Add the onion, ginger and garlic and sauté for 8 minutes until softened, taking care not to let them burn. Add the refried beans, vegetable stock and most of the tomatoes, then bring to the boil. Reduce the heat and simmer until almost all of the stock has evaporated away. Season well, to taste.

Plate up the sweet potato halves and spoon over the refried bean mixture. Halve the avocados, remove the stones and spoon the flesh on top of the beans. Scatter over the remaining cherry tomatoes, the dried chilli and the coriander leaves. Season with a little more salt and pepper and a drizzle of olive oil. Serve immediately.

ROOT VEGETABLE MASH

These two mash recipes transform humble root veg into something special.
They're the perfect side dishes to serve with the Festive Roast on page 142.

CARROT AND TURNIP MASH

SERVES 4–6

8 medium carrots, peeled and roughly chopped

2 medium turnips, peeled and roughly chopped

60g non-dairy butter or 60ml extra virgin olive oil

Sea salt and freshly ground black pepper, to taste

Put the carrots and turnips in a large pan and cover them with cold water. Add a teaspoon of salt and bring to the boil, then reduce the heat a little and simmer for 20–30 minutes until completely tender – the tip of a knife should glide into the thickest part of the vegetables without any resistance. Drain well and tip the vegetables back into the hot pan to steam dry – off the heat – for a further 10 minutes.

Transfer the vegetables to a food processor and add the butter or oil. Blitz until smooth, then season to taste with salt and pepper. Alternatively, if you prefer a chunkier consistency, mash the vegetables with a hand masher.

PURÉED PARSNIPS

SERVES 4

6 medium parsnips, peeled and roughly chopped

20g non-dairy butter

1 tsp fresh thyme leaves

1 tsp vegan mustard

1 tbsp unsweetened, plant-based milk of your choice

Sea salt and freshly ground black pepper, to taste

Place the parsnips in a large saucepan and cover them with cold water. Add a teaspoon of salt and bring to the boil. Reduce the heat a little and simmer the parsnips for 20–30 minutes until completely tender – the tip of a knife should glide into the thickest part of the vegetables without any resistance. Drain well and then tip them back into the hot pan to steam dry for a further 10 minutes.

Transfer the dry parsnips to a food processor, add the butter, thyme, mustard and milk, then blitz until smooth. Season to taste with salt and pepper. Alternatively, if you prefer a chunkier consistency, mash the parsnips by hand. Add a little more milk or butter if desired and serve immediately.

GARLIC BREAD

Who can resist the wonderful aroma of freshly baked garlic bread? This recipe turns a simple bowl of soup or salad into a feast. Also great served with the stew on page 168.

SERVES 6–8

1 baguette

75ml extra virgin olive oil

2 medium garlic cloves, peeled and crushed

2 tbsp very finely chopped flatleaf parsley

Sea salt and freshly ground black pepper, to taste

Preheat the oven to 180°C/Fan 160°C/Gas 4.

Make diagonal cuts at 3cm intervals all along the baguette, making sure you don't cut the whole way through the bread. Mix the olive oil, garlic and parsley in a bowl and season generously with salt and pepper.

Gently pull each cut apart and use a teaspoon to spread a little of the garlic and parsley oil on to each side of each slice of bread. Keep going until you have used up all the flavoured oil.

Wrap the baguette in foil and bake it in the oven for 10 minutes until heated through. Serve immediately.

TANGY WINTER GREENS

Dark green vegetables are packed with so many health benefits, and this is a great way of giving them some extra punch. You could also add a teaspoon each of ground coriander, cumin seeds and mustard seeds to the hot oil if you want your greens extra spicy. This serves four as a side and it's also delicious on top of cooked quinoa or rice as a main course.

SERVES 4

4 tbsp extra virgin olive oil

3 medium garlic cloves, peeled and crushed

2cm piece of fresh root ginger, peeled and finely grated

1 red chilli, deseeded and finely chopped (optional)

200g cavolo nero, stalks removed and leaves roughly chopped

150g rainbow chard, stalks and leaves roughly chopped

150ml coconut milk or unsweetened plant-based milk of your choice

Zest and juice of 1 lime

Sea salt and freshly ground black pepper, to taste

To serve

1 tsp dried chilli flakes, to taste (optional)

Put the oil into a large pan with a lid and place over a medium-high heat. Once the oil is hot, add the garlic, ginger and the fresh chilli, if using. Fry, stirring now and again, for 1–3 minutes. Take great care not to burn the garlic.

Add the cavolo nero, chard and coconut milk and season generously to taste with salt and pepper. Stir to combine, cover with the lid and steam for 4 minutes, then remove the lid and continue to cook for another 1–2 minutes until the leaves are wilted and the sauce has reduced down.

Add the lime zest and juice, stir to combine, taste again and adjust the seasoning if necessary. Serve with the dried chilli scattered over the top, if you like.

PREP
10

COOK
20

CHARGRILLED CABBAGE WITH THAI DRESSING AND CASHEW NUTS

Cabbage is cheap, available everywhere and great to eat – it's good brain food too. Try this way of serving it with a delicious tangy Thai dressing. The cashew nuts add a lovely crunchy finishing touch.

SERVES 4

1 large pointed spring cabbage, outer leaves removed and quartered lengthways

3 tbsp olive oil

Sea salt and freshly ground black pepper, to taste

Thai dressing

Large bunch of fresh coriander

2cm piece of fresh root ginger, peeled

2 garlic cloves, peeled

1 red chilli, deseeded

1 tbsp coconut palm or brown sugar

2 tsp soy sauce or tamari

2½ tbsp fresh lime juice

To serve

Small handful of roasted, salted cashew nuts

For the Thai dressing, cut the stems off the bunch of coriander (reserve the leaves for the garnish) and put them in a food processor. Add the ginger, garlic and chilli and blitz until very finely chopped. Then add the sugar, soy sauce and lime juice and blitz to combine. Taste and, if necessary, adjust the seasoning with a little more sugar or soy sauce.

Coat the cabbage quarters in oil and season well. Place them on a hot griddle pan and reduce the heat to medium. Cover with a lid or tin foil and fry for 5–6 minutes on all sides, until charred and tender.

Serve the cabbage with the Thai sauce drizzled on top and the cashew nuts and some of the coriander leaves scattered over the top.

"

YEARS AGO, OUR
MOTHERS USED TO
THINK THAT THE ONLY
WAY YOU COULD GET
ENOUGH PROTEIN,
VITAMINS AND MINERALS
WAS BY EATING MEAT. BUT
TIMES HAVE CHANGED.

"

Linda McCartney — 1989

DAL WITH COURGETTE AND CHILLI

Dal is an excellent standby that can be served with curries or on its own with rice or nan bread for a quick warming meal. The cooking time of lentils does vary, so check the packet instructions and be prepared to cook for longer or add more water to get the result you want. Some like a soupy dal, others prefer a drier dish – the joy of making your own dal is that you can have it just the way you like it.

SERVES 4–6
AS A SIDE DISH

240g split red lentils

3 medium garlic cloves, peeled and crushed

3cm piece of fresh root ginger, peeled and finely grated

1 medium courgette, trimmed and coarsely grated

2 tbsp soy sauce or tamari

1 tsp ground coriander

1 tsp ground cumin

4 tbsp unsweetened non-dairy yoghurt

1 tbsp apple cider vinegar

Sea salt and freshly ground black pepper, to taste

To serve

1 tsp dried chilli flakes

1 tbsp extra virgin olive oil

Unsweetened non-dairy yoghurt

Wash the lentils under cold running water. Put them in a pan with the garlic, ginger, courgette, soy sauce and spices and cover with 700ml of water. Bring to the boil, then reduce the heat to low and simmer gently for 20 minutes, stirring frequently, until most of the water has been absorbed and the lentils are almost creamy.

Add the 4 tablespoons of yoghurt and simmer for another 5 minutes until you have a creamy dal. Stir in the apple cider vinegar and season to taste.

Serve the dal in bowls with the dried chilli scattered over the top, a drizzle of olive oil and a dollop of yoghurt.

GREEN BEANS WITH RED ONION AND DILL

A plant-based diet is good for your health and for the health of the planet – and it's so delicious too. Simple things like adding a few extras to beautiful green beans elevates this side dish to something even more special.

SERVES 6

500g French or runner
  beans, trimmed
  and halved

3 tbsp fresh dill,
  finely chopped

1 small red onion, peeled
  and very finely chopped

1 large garlic clove, peeled
  and crushed

30g capers, rinsed

Sea salt and freshly
  ground black pepper,
  to taste

Dressing

1 tsp mustard

2 tsp fresh lemon juice

1½ tbsp balsamic vinegar

4 tbsp extra virgin olive oil

For the dressing, put the mustard, lemon juice, vinegar and oil into a bowl and whisk together. Season to taste.

Steam or boil the beans for 3–5 minutes, until vibrant green and a little more tender, but still crisp.

While the beans are still warm, toss them with the dill, red onion, garlic, capers and the dressing. Season to taste and serve immediately.

POSH SAUSAGE ROLLS

Absolutely delish – these rolls have a sophisticated filling wrapped in crumbly pastry and they're great served with tomato ketchup or barbecue sauce to dip. The recipe includes how to make the vegan sausages, but if you don't have time you can bake pre-made Linda McCartney vegetarian sausages instead. Any mushrooms are fine, but the shiitake kind do add lots of great flavour if you can find them.

MAKES 20 ROLLS

3 tbsp olive oil, plus
   extra for frying

1 medium onion, peeled
   and finely chopped

250g mushrooms, such
   as button or shiitake,
   very finely chopped

3 medium garlic cloves,
   peeled and crushed

1 tsp chopped thyme leaves

2 tsp finely chopped fresh
   rosemary leaves

400g tin of kidney beans,
   drained and rinsed

1 tsp sweet smoked paprika

100g ground almonds

150g smoked tofu, drained
   and grated

3 tbsp white spelt or plain
   white flour, sifted, plus
   extra to dust

Put the 3 tablespoons of oil into a pan and place over a medium heat. Add the onion and mushrooms and cook gently for 12–15 minutes until the mushrooms have released all their liquid and it has evaporated away. Add the garlic, thyme and most of the rosemary and fry for another 2 minutes until aromatic. Season to taste.

Put the kidney beans into a food processor and blitz into a rough paste. Transfer to a bowl and stir in the mushroom mixture, smoked paprika, ground almonds, tofu and flour. Season generously to taste.

Divide the mixture into 10 portions of equal size. The most accurate way to do this is to weigh the whole mixture and divide it by 10. Shape each portion into a sausage shape, compacting it firmly with your hands. Fry the sausages in a little oil over a medium heat, turning now and then until golden. Transfer to a plate and leave to cool.

When you are ready to make the sausage rolls, preheat the oven to 200°C/Fan 180°C/Gas 6 and line a baking tray with baking paper.

Roll out the pastry on a floured surface to a rectangle measuring about 50 x 30cm. Cut the pastry in half lengthways, and then divide each long strip of pastry into 10 pieces of equal size.

Cut the 10 sausages in half and place each half on top of a piece of pastry. Brush one end of the pastry with a little soya milk, then roll it up, encasing the sausage inside. Lightly press the end of the pastry to seal. Continue with the remaining rolls and place them on the baking tray.

500g ready-made vegan
  puff pastry

Soya milk, to brush

Sea salt and freshly ground
  black pepper, to taste

To serve

Ketchup or barbecue sauce

Brush each roll with a little more milk, then scatter over the rest of
the chopped rosemary and lightly season with salt and pepper. Bake
for 25–30 minutes until deeply golden and well risen. Leave to cool
for 5 minutes before serving with ketchup or barbecue sauce.

I wasn't surprised that Linda became such an enthusiastic cook. For her, home and family were so important, and cooking was part of that. As a family, we were raised with a love of food – something that came from our dad, who was a big lover of life in all ways. I remember that one summer we went to Switzerland and tasted Lindt chocolate for the first time. You couldn't get it at home then, so my dad arranged to have some shipped to us once a month.

When we were growing up, the diet in the US was quite plain, not as interesting and varied as it is today. Nothing was very fancy, but we used to holiday out on Cape Cod where we went to a wonderful restaurant in Provincetown – it's still there. We would eat things like eggplant parmesan and really good tomato sauce and then go home and make our own versions.

We all liked to cook, but Linda was the keenest. She was an intuitive cook and knew how to put things together to taste good. It was all very easy-going but wonderful.

Louise

Sister to Linda

PREP
10

COOK
40

CURRIED LENTILS

Puy lentils are best here, as they keep their shape well. This is lovely served just as it is, or you can pile the lentils on to a bed of cooked greens or salad leaves to make a main meal. Any leftovers can be added to a salad the next day.

SERVES 4

2 tbsp extra virgin olive oil, plus extra to drizzle

2 medium onions, peeled and finely chopped

2 medium garlic cloves, peeled and crushed

1–2 tbsp curry powder, to taste, plus extra to serve

1 tsp ground cumin

225g puy lentils

600ml vegetable stock or water

Zest of 1 lemon and 2 tbsp lemon juice

8 cherry tomatoes, quartered

1 tbsp non-dairy crème fraîche, to serve

2 tbsp roughly chopped flatleaf parsley leaves

Sea salt and freshly ground black pepper, to taste

Put the oil in a large saucepan and place over a medium-high heat. Add the onions and sauté for 8 minutes until they begin to soften, then add the garlic and spices and cook for another 2 minutes until aromatic. Add the lentils and cook for another 2 minutes, stirring now and again.

Add the stock or water, lemon zest and juice and bring to the boil, then reduce the heat and season to taste, bearing in mind your stock may already be salted. Cook the lentils for 20–25 minutes until tender, but still retaining a little bite. Remove the lid, add the tomatoes and cook for another 2–5 minutes until almost all the cooking liquid has evaporated.

Remove the pan from the heat and adjust the seasoning if necessary. Transfer to a bowl, spoon over the crème fraîche and scatter over the parsley and a pinch of the curry powder.

Drizzle with a little more olive oil and serve hot as a side or at room temperature as part of a salad.

GRIDDLED VEGETABLES WITH HARISSA

Cooking vegetables on a griddle makes them extra sweet and delicious, with a wonderful charred flavour, and serving them with the vibrant harissa paste turns them into a really exciting side dish. You can also cook the vegetables on a barbecue.

SERVES 4

Harissa paste

2½ tsp coriander seeds

2½ tsp cumin seeds

1 tsp caraway seeds

½ tsp ground cinnamon

4 tbsp extra virgin olive oil, plus extra if desired

1 medium red onion, peeled and quartered

2 red chillies, deseeded

3 garlic cloves, peeled

1 roasted red pepper, from a jar, drained

1 tbsp tomato purée

2 tbsp fresh lemon juice

1 tsp sweet smoked paprika

Sea salt and freshly ground black pepper, to taste

Griddled vegetables

Assorted vegetables, such as courgettes, aubergines, onions, pointed cabbage, asparagus, mushrooms

Extra virgin olive oil

To serve

Flatleaf parsley leaves

Gently toast the coriander, cumin and caraway seeds in a dry frying pan until they are a shade darker and aromatic. Use a pestle and mortar or coffee grinder to pound or blitz them until finely ground. Tip into a bowl, add the ground cinnamon and set aside.

In the same pan, heat a tablespoon of the oil and sauté the onion and chillies for 8 minutes over a medium-low heat, until softened. Add the garlic and fry for another 1–2 minutes until aromatic.

Put the onion mixture, ground spices, remaining 3 tablespoons of oil and the rest of the harissa ingredients into a food processor and blitz until smooth. Add a little more olive oil or water if you prefer a thinner consistency for drizzling. Season with salt and pepper to taste, cover and set aside.

Cut the thicker vegetables, such as courgettes, aubergines, onions and pointed cabbage, into 1–2cm thick slices or wedges. Thinner or smaller vegetables like asparagus or small mushrooms can be left whole. Put the prepared vegetables into a large bowl and drizzle over 2–3 tablespoons of olive oil, just enough to coat everything. Season generously with salt and pepper and gently toss until evenly coated.

Place a griddle pan over a medium-high heat. Add the vegetables to the pan in batches, so as not to overcrowd the pan. Cook the vegetables for 3–6 minutes on each side, depending on the thickness, until golden and softened. Bear in mind that some vegetables will take longer than others, so keep a close eye on them, transferring any cooked vegetables to a plate while you carry on with the rest.

When ready to serve, arrange all the vegetables on a platter, drizzle over the harissa and scatter over some parsley. Serve immediately.

PREP
5

COOK
20

TOMATO SAUCE

You can use this classic tomato sauce as a topping for pizzas (see page 162), with pasta or however you like. You can also add vegan mince to make it into a bolognese sauce. It's worth making double the quantity and stashing some away in the freezer for a day when you're short of time.

SERVES 4–6

3 garlic cloves, peeled
and thinly sliced

2 x 400g tins of chopped
tomatoes

4 tbsp extra virgin olive oil

2 tsp balsamic vinegar

1 tsp sea salt

4 sprigs of basil

Put all the ingredients into a pan and place over a high heat. The moment they begin to bubble and splutter, turn the heat down to low and simmer the sauce gently for 20 minutes, stirring frequently, until slightly thickened.

Remove the sauce from the heat and leave to cool for 5 minutes. Use a hand-held blender or a food processor to purée the sauce until completely smooth. Transfer to an airtight container and leave to cool completely. Keep refrigerated until ready to use.

BAKING

IRISH SODA BREAD

Soda bread is a quick bread to make because it is traditionally made without yeast, so does not require time to rise. Usually it includes buttermilk, the acidity of which reacts with the bicarbonate of soda to keep the bread light and airy. Here, we use a combination of lemon juice or vinegar and plant-based milk to do the same job. The bread must be baked soon after mixing or the bubbles will deflate and the result will be heavy.

MAKES 1 LOAF

Non-dairy butter, to grease

250ml unsweetened plant-based milk of your choice

1½ tbsp fresh lemon juice or apple cider vinegar

55g wholewheat flour

225g white spelt or plain flour, plus extra to dust

55g rolled oats

1 tsp fine sea salt

1½ tsp bicarbonate of soda

Preheat the oven to 220°C/Fan 200°C/Gas 7. Lightly grease a baking tray with non-dairy butter.

Pour the milk into a measuring jug and stir in the lemon juice or vinegar. Put all the remaining dry ingredients into a large bowl and mix. Make a well in the centre and add most of the milk mixture. Stir with a wooden spoon, adding more of the remaining milk if the mixture seems too dry. It should be quite a moist and sticky dough, but not too wet.

Dust your hands and your baking tray with flour and transfer the dough to the tray. Pat the dough into a round of about 15–16cm in diameter. Make a cross in the top of the loaf with a sharp, floured knife, but don't cut the whole way through.

Bake the loaf for 15 minutes, then reduce the heat to 200°C/Fan 180°C/Gas 6. Bake for another 10 minutes until the loaf is brown and sounds hollow when tapped on the base. Transfer to a wire rack and leave to cool completely.

BROWN BREAD SANDWICH LOAF

This is a traditional bread that needs yeast for the dough to rise. It's easy to make and there's nothing better than the smell of bread baking. A delicious loaf for toast, sandwiches or just spread generously with peanut butter and jelly (jam) – Linda's favourite.

MAKES 1 LARGE LOAF

Olive oil, to grease

400g wholemeal bread flour, plus extra to dust

200g wholegrain spelt flour, or more wholegrain wheat flour

10g salt

2 tsp unrefined or caster sugar

10g fast-action dried yeast

30ml olive oil, plus extra for greasing

200ml soya milk

200ml warm water

Grease a 23 x 13cm loaf tin and set it aside. Place all the ingredients in a large mixing bowl and mix with a wooden spoon, until no dry flour remains visible. Cover loosely and leave to one side for 15 minutes in a warm spot in the kitchen.

If you have a stand mixer fitted with a kneading paddle, transfer the dough to the mixer and knead for 6 or 7 minutes until it is elastic and stretchy with a smooth sheen to it. If kneading by hand, this may take up to 15 minutes. Place the dough in a bowl, cover and leave to prove for 1 hour, or until doubled in size.

Punch the dough to knock out the air and turn it out on to a lightly floured work surface. Flatten the dough into a rough oblong shape, about the length of your tin, then tightly roll up the dough, starting from the widest side. Transfer the dough to your tin, making sure the seam of the roll is facing down and the smooth surface is facing up. Brush with a little water, cover loosely and leave to rise for 20–40 minutes, until it has risen about 1–2cm above the edge of your tin.

While the dough is rising, preheat the oven to 240°C/Fan 220°C/Gas 9. When the dough has risen, put the loaf in the oven and immediately turn the temperature down to 220°C/Fan 200°C/Gas 7. Bake for 30 minutes until golden.

Remove the loaf from its tin and return to the oven for 10–15 minutes until deeply golden brown and the base sounds hollow when lightly tapped with your finger. Leave to cool completely on a wire rack.

LEMON DRIZZLE CAKE

Bursting with the fresh flavour of lemons, this loaf cake uses both the juice and the yellow zest for flavour impact. Flax seeds work like magic to bind the mixture and give your baked goods structure. The seeds just need to be soaked in hot water and then whisked into the mixture, in the same way as beaten eggs.

SERVES 6

125g non-dairy butter,
    at room temperature,
    plus extra to grease

2 tbsp milled flax seeds

6 tbsp warm water

150g unrefined or
    caster sugar

Zest of 2 lemons and
    4 tbsp lemon juice

180g white spelt or
    plain flour

2 tsp baking powder

4 tbsp unsweetened plant-
    based milk, such as soya

60g icing sugar, sifted

Preheat the oven to 180°C/Fan 160°C/Gas 4. Grease a loaf tin (one measuring about 9 x 13.5 x 25cm) with a little non-dairy butter and line it with baking paper.

Put the flax seeds into a large bowl with the warm water and set aside to thicken and cool.

Put the sugar, butter and lemon zest into a bowl and beat with an electric whisk until pale, light and fluffy. Gradually whisk in the cooled flax seed mixture, then, using a spatula, fold in the flour and baking powder. Add 2 tablespoons of the lemon juice and the milk and beat into the mixture.

Scoop the mixture into the loaf tin and bake for 45 minutes until golden and firm to the touch. Open the oven door to let the heat escape, but leave the cake where it is for 5 minutes. This helps to prevent the cake from sinking.

Remove the cake from the oven. Mix the remaining lemon juice with the icing sugar until smooth, then make holes in the top of the cake with a skewer and drizzle over the lemon and sugar mixture. Leave the cake to cool in the tin for 30 minutes, then gently turn it out on to a wire rack to cool completely. Serve in thick slices.

Mum was a tactile cook. She enjoyed the colour and variety of vegetables and fruit, but she didn't want to handle meat. I think that was one of the reasons why she became vegetarian. Her food was packed with flavour and she found cooking relaxing and inspiring. She added little touches that transformed a dish – a squeeze of lemon here, some fresh herbs there. Her food was comfort food, quite hearty, and she described herself as a peasant cook. She wasn't one for measuring or exact quantities and she liked recipes to be simple and accessible, without tricky ingredients that you had to search the shops for.

She was – and still is – a huge influence on the way I eat. I grew up talking about food with the family and I'm still like that. I'll have just finished breakfast and I'll be thinking about what to eat for lunch or dinner.

My favourite dessert was Mum's rice pudding and she also baked great brownies and lemon drizzle cake – things I still make today.

Mary

RICH FRUIT CAKE

A traditional fruit cake, packed with dried fruit, nuts and seeds, this makes an excellent treat and can be made well in advance. It's perfect served with an afternoon cup of tea or it can be decorated beautifully for a special occasion. As with the lemon drizzle cake on page 206, flax seeds take on the role of eggs in this recipe.

SERVES 10–12

225g non-dairy butter, plus extra to grease

4 tbsp milled flax seeds

100ml warm water

115g caster sugar

115g muscovado brown sugar

Zest and juice of 1 lemon

Zest and juice of 1 orange

100g glacé cherries, chopped

275g raisins

275g sultanas

275g currants

100g mixed peel, finely chopped

150ml whisky, or more orange juice if you prefer

2 tsp mixed spice

1 tsp ground cinnamon

200g self-raising flour

150g almonds, roughly chopped

100g pumpkin seeds

Preheat the oven to 150°C/Fan 130°C/Gas 2. Grease a 23cm round cake tin with non-dairy butter and double line it with baking paper. Tie a double layer of brown paper around the outside of the tin. This prevents the sides of the tin getting too hot during the long cooking time and scorching the cake.

Put the milled flax seeds into a large bowl with the warm water. Stir to combine and set aside.

Put the non-dairy butter, sugars, lemon and orange zest and juice, cherries, raisins, sultanas, currants, mixed peel and whisky into a large saucepan and bring to the boil. As soon as it reaches the boil, reduce the temperature and simmer for 5 minutes, stirring regularly. Transfer to a bowl and leave to cool.

Once cool, stir in the flax seed mixture, mixed spice, cinnamon, flour, almonds and pumpkin seeds. Transfer the mixture to the prepared tin and bake for 2 hours and 15 minutes, until a skewer comes out mostly clean. Cover the cake with foil if it is browning too quickly. Remove and leave the cake to cool in the tin before turning out. Discard the paper.

Store in an airtight container in a cool place – this cake can be made up to a month in advance. Serve as it is or with royal icing or any form of decoration you like on top.

BANANA CAKE

Bananas are an excellent source of potassium and make a handy snack. This cake is a perfect use for overripe bananas, which have a more intense flavour than usual – and they are easier to mash.

SERVES 8

115g non-dairy butter,
    at room temperature,
    plus extra to grease

2 tbsp milled flax seeds

5 tbsp warm water

150g unrefined or
    caster sugar

3 ripe Fairtrade bananas,
    peeled and mashed

2 tsp vanilla extract

2 tbsp non-dairy plain
    yoghurt (coconut
    works well)

1 tsp apple cider vinegar

225g white spelt or plain
    flour or gluten-free flour

1 tsp bicarbonate of soda

1 tsp baking powder

1½ tsp ground cinnamon

150g pecan nuts, roughly
    chopped (optional)

To serve

50g icing sugar

Slices of dried banana
    (optional)

Preheat the oven to 180°C/Fan 160°C/Gas 4. Grease a 20cm round cake tin with a little non-dairy butter and line it with baking paper.

Put the flax seeds into a large bowl with the warm water. Stir to combine and set aside.

In a bowl, beat the butter and the sugar with an electric whisk until pale, light and fluffy. Whisk in the flax mixture, mashed bananas, vanilla extract, yoghurt and vinegar. Then gradually fold in the flour, bicarbonate of soda, baking powder, cinnamon and half the pecan nuts, if using, until thoroughly combined.

Transfer the mixture to the cake tin and scatter over the remaining pecan nuts, if using. Bake for 30–35 minutes until the cake is just firm and a skewer comes out mostly clean. Remove and leave to cool for 5 minutes, then turn out on to a wire rack to cool completely.

To serve, mix the icing sugar with 1–2 tablespoons of water. Drizzle this mixture over the cake and scatter a few slices of dried banana over the top, if you like.

CHOCOLATE AND HAZELNUT BROWNIES

When Linda made a batch of her brownies they would be devoured within minutes. Irresistible. These brownies are gooey and mouth-wateringly good and so easy to make. The hazelnuts add extra crunch and flavour.

MAKES 12 BROWNIES

100g non-dairy butter or odourless coconut oil, at room temperature, plus extra to grease

2 tbsp milled flax seeds

6 tbsp warm water

100g dark chocolate, 70% cocoa, roughly chopped

200g unrefined or caster sugar

1 tsp vanilla extract

100g white spelt or plain flour

1 tsp baking powder

60g hazelnuts, halved, plus extra to scatter on top (optional)

½ tsp fine sea salt

Preheat the oven to 180°C/Fan 160°C/Gas 4. Grease a 20cm square cake tin with some non-dairy butter or coconut oil and line it with baking paper.

Put the flax seeds into a large bowl with the warm water. Stir to combine and set aside.

Put the chocolate into a heatproof bowl and place it over a pan of barely simmering water. Make sure the bottom of the bowl does not come into contact with the water. Stir the chocolate every now and again until it has melted.

In a separate bowl, beat the non-dairy butter or coconut oil, sugar and vanilla with an electric whisk until light and fluffy. With the whisk still on, whisk in the melted chocolate until fully combined, then stir in the flax seed mixture.

Use a spatula to fold the flour, baking powder, hazelnuts and salt into the chocolate mixture. Transfer to the lined tin and scatter with extra hazelnuts, if using. Bake for 20–25 minutes, until the brownies are just set, but still a little gooey in the centre. Remove from the oven and leave to cool completely. Slice into squares and serve, or store in an airtight container.

PREP
15

COOK
30

GINGERBREAD CAKE

Gingerbread is a much-loved classic bake and this dairy-free version is wonderfully squidgy, sticky and satisfying. This is great just as it is or, when served with some plant-based vanilla ice cream, it makes a delightful pudding.

SERVES 6

120g non-dairy butter, plus extra to grease

1 tbsp milled flax seeds

3 tbsp warm water

120g unrefined or caster sugar

225g white spelt, plain white flour or gluten-free flour, sifted

1 tsp baking powder

1 tsp bicarbonate of soda

1 tsp ground cinnamon

1 tsp ground ginger

¼ tsp ground nutmeg

120ml unsweetened plant-based milk of your choice

2 tbsp blackstrap molasses or treacle

To serve

Maple syrup

Non-dairy yoghurt or cream

Preheat the oven to 180°C/Fan 160°C/Gas 4. Grease an 18cm round cake tin with non-dairy butter and line with baking paper.

Put the flax seeds into a bowl with the warm water and set aside.

In a large bowl, cream together the non-dairy butter and sugar with an electric whisk until light and fluffy. Fold in the flax seed mixture, flour, baking powder, bicarbonate of soda, cinnamon, ginger, nutmeg and milk until smooth. Gently heat the molasses or treacle until runny, then fold into the batter.

Transfer the batter to the cake tin and bake for 25–30 minutes, until a skewer inserted into the centre comes out clean. Remove and leave to cool for 10 minutes, then turn out on to a wire rack to cool completely. Serve with a drizzle of maple syrup and non-dairy yoghurt or cream.

CARROT CAKE

When folded into cake batter, sweet root vegetables, such as carrots and beetroot, give a lusciously moist result and this example is no exception. It's nutritious and topped with a citrus and maple syrup frosting to complete the flavour sensation.

SERVES 10

250ml vegetable oil, plus extra for greasing

3 tbsp milled flax seeds

130ml warm water

220g coconut palm sugar or light muscovado sugar

300g white spelt or plain flour

2 tsp baking powder

200g carrots, peeled and coarsely grated

40g walnuts, chopped

40g pecans, chopped

1½ tsp ground cinnamon

1½ tsp mixed spice

1 tsp ground ginger

Zest of 1 medium orange

Icing

350g non-dairy cream cheese

2 tbsp maple syrup

Zest of 1 medium orange

Zest of 1 lemon

Preheat the oven to 180°C/Fan 160°C/Gas 4. Grease two 20cm round cake tins with vegetable oil and line with baking paper.

Put the milled flax seeds into a bowl with the warm water, mix well and set aside.

For the icing, put the cream cheese and maple syrup into a bowl with the orange and lemon zest and mix together. Cover and refrigerate.

For the cake, put the milled flax mixture, sugar and oil into a large bowl and mix together. Fold in the flour, baking powder, carrots, nuts, cinnamon, mixed spice, ground ginger and orange zest.

Divide the mixture between the two cake tins and bake for 20–25 minutes, until a skewer comes out clean. Remove from the oven and leave to cool completely.

Place one layer of cake on a plate and ice with half the icing. Place the second layer on top and ice again.

> # FISH, CHICKEN AND LAMB ALL HAVE HEARTS AND EYES AND FEELINGS AND BABIES JUST LIKE THE HUMAN ANIMAL.

Linda McCartney – 1995

PECAN, HEMP AND RAISIN FLAPJACKS

Hemp seeds are hailed by many as a superfood, as they are rich in protein, fibre, good fats and vitamins and minerals. Combined with oats, nuts and dried fruit, they make really yummy flapjacks that taste good and do you good. They're perfect as a snack on the go or as part of a packed lunch.

MAKES 12–16 FLAPJACKS

140g coconut oil, plus extra to grease

120g coconut palm or light brown muscovado sugar

2 tbsp maple or golden syrup

200g rolled oats

60g pecans, roughly chopped

60g raisins or chopped unsulphured dried apricots

60g hulled hemp seeds

½ tsp ground cinnamon (optional)

Preheat the oven to 180°C/Fan 160°C/Gas 4. Grease a 16 x 24cm baking tray with a little coconut oil and line it with baking paper.

Put the coconut oil, sugar and syrup into a pan and place over a medium heat. Stir now and again until everything has completely melted, then remove from the heat.

Put 60g of the oats into a food processor and grind them down to a powder. Add this to the pan of melted coconut oil and sugar, together with the remaining oats, the pecans, raisins or apricots, hemp seeds and cinnamon, if using. Stir until thoroughly combined.

Transfer to the baking tin and smooth out, then very firmly flatten and compact the mixture with the back of a spoon. Bake for 20–25 minutes until golden. Remove and leave to cool completely, then slice into squares or rectangles. Store in an airtight container for up to 3 days.

CRUNCHY PECAN COOKIES

Simple to make, these have a crisp, crunchy coating and a chewy inside, with a tantalising hint of orange and vanilla flavour. Like all nuts, pecans are a good source of protein and healthy fats, and they also contain vitamins and antioxidants.

MAKES 20 COOKIES

140g pecan nuts,
    finely chopped

100g non-dairy butter,
    at room temperature

120g self-raising flour

90g unrefined or
    caster sugar

Zest of ½ orange

1 tsp vanilla extract

Icing sugar, to dust

Put all the ingredients, except the icing sugar, in a large bowl and beat together until thoroughly combined. Bring together into a ball of dough, then take heaped teaspoons of the mixture and roll into balls. Place these on a tray and leave them in the fridge for 30 minutes.

Meanwhile, preheat the oven to 200°C/Fan 180°C/Gas 6 and line a couple of baking sheets with baking paper.

Place the cookies on the baking trays, leaving at least 3cm around each one. Bake for 15–18 minutes until lightly golden. Remove the cookies and dust each one with icing sugar while still hot, then leave to cool. Store in an airtight container.

COCONUT AND CHERRY BITES

Coconut and cherry is a classic combination and these delectable little treats are a cross between a biscuit and a macaroon with a beautiful nutty flavour. You can use gluten-free flour for a gluten-free option.

MAKES 24

90g cashew or almond nut butter

40ml coconut oil, melted

230g desiccated coconut

80g dried cherries or other dried fruit

Pinch of sea salt

Zest of 1 lime and 1 tbsp juice

110ml maple syrup

2 tbsp white spelt, plain or gluten-free flour

1 tsp bicarbonate of soda

Preheat the oven to 180°C/Fan 160°C/Gas 4 and line a baking sheet with greaseproof paper.

Put the cashew butter and coconut oil into a large pan and place over a low heat. Stir frequently until just melted. Take care not to let the mixture come to the boil.

Remove from the heat, add all the remaining ingredients and mix together until thoroughly combined. The mixture will be quite dry, but persevere until everything is mixed together.

Place 2 tablespoons of the mixture, about 20g, into the palm of your hand and compress to form a ball. Lightly flatten the top and bottom of the ball and place it on a baking sheet. The mixture is quite fragile uncooked, so don't worry if it breaks a little bit, just push it back together once positioned on the baking tray. These will stick together once cooked and cooled. Continue with the rest of the mixture, leaving a 2cm gap between each ball. Bake for 8 minutes, until lightly golden.

Remove from the oven and leave to cool completely to firm up. Store in an airtight container in the fridge for up to a week.

PUDDINGS
AND
SWEET
TREATS

NO-BAKE CHOCOLATE, PISTACHIO AND CRANBERRY SQUARES

These are so good you might want to hide them away and keep them for yourself! And there's no real cooking, other than melting the chocolate – just a bit of stirring, mixing and bashing. Once set, these have a delectable flavour and texture that's impossible to resist.

MAKES 16 SQUARES

60g coconut oil, plus
    extra to grease
250g dark chocolate, 70%
    cocoa, roughly chopped
1 tbsp maple syrup
120g vegan biscuits,
    chocolate or plain,
    roughly chopped
40g cranberries or raisins
40g dates, pitted and
    roughly chopped
80g roasted pistachios,
    roughly chopped

Grease a 20cm square cake tin with some coconut oil and line it with baking paper.

Put the coconut oil, chocolate and maple syrup into a heatproof bowl and place it over a pan of barely simmering water. Make sure the bottom of the bowl doesn't touch the water. Stir the mixture every now and again until melted.

Pour about three-quarters of the chocolate mixture into a large mixing bowl. Keep the remaining melted chocolate over the pan of hot water but turn off the heat.

Add the biscuits, cranberries or raisins, dates and most of the pistachios to the mixing bowl and stir to combine. Transfer the mixture to the lined tin and flatten it out. Working very quickly, pour over the remaining melted chocolate and smooth it over. Sprinkle over the remaining pistachios.

Cover and refrigerate until it has completely set, then remove and cut into squares. Serve or keep stored in the fridge in an airtight container.

STICKY TOFFEE PUDDINGS

Blackstrap molasses, coconut sugar and dates bring a rich, sweet depth of flavour to these wonderfully tempting little puddings. A drizzle of toffee sauce provides a delicious finishing touch. Dessert heaven!

SERVES 8

100g non-dairy butter, plus extra to grease

3 tbsp milled flax seeds

130ml warm water

220g pitted dates, chopped

100ml soya milk

150g coconut palm sugar or light brown sugar

2 tbsp blackstrap molasses or treacle

2 tsp vanilla extract

Pinch of salt

180g plain flour (or gluten-free flour mix)

1½ tsp baking powder

Sauce

120g coconut palm sugar or light brown sugar

100g non-dairy butter

120ml soya or oat cream, plus extra to serve

1 tbsp blackstrap molasses or treacle

Preheat the oven to 200°C/Fan 180°C/Gas 6. Grease and line the base of 8 mini pudding or dariole moulds with non-dairy butter. Put the flax seeds in a bowl with the warm water, mix and set aside.

Put the dates and 100ml of water in a saucepan and bring to the boil. Reduce the heat and simmer for 3–5 minutes until the dates are completely soft.

Place the date and water mixture in a food processor and blitz until smooth. Add the milk, butter, sugar, molasses, flax mixture, vanilla and a good pinch of salt and blitz again until well combined. Transfer to a bowl and fold in the flour and baking powder.

Divide the mixture between the moulds. Bake for 18–22 minutes or until they have risen and are just set. A skewer should come out clean. If they look like they are beginning to burn, cover with foil.

Remove the puddings and leave them to cool for 10 minutes, then trim off the rounded top, so they sit flat on a plate when turned out. Gently remove them from the tins and transfer to plates.

While the puddings are in the oven, make the sauce. Place the sugar, butter and cream in a saucepan over a medium heat and cook until the sugar has dissolved. Add the molasses or treacle and cook for another 4–5 minutes, stirring all the time, until the mixture has thickened and darkened in colour. Serve the puddings with the toffee sauce and some more cream.

KEY LIME PIE

Avocados give the vibrant lime-green filling of this pie a wonderful silky smoothness and there's a hint of coconut flavour too. The crisp biscuit base contains dates to help bind it together and provides a perfect contrast in texture. It's important to keep this in the fridge until ready to serve to ensure it stays set, and you can store it for up to three days.

SERVES 10–12

Base
Vegetable oil, to grease
250g vegan digestive biscuits
100g coconut oil, melted
90g pitted medjool dates
Pinch of sea salt

Topping
225g ripe avocado flesh, approximately 2 large avocados
200g tinned coconut cream
1½ tbsp cornflour
125ml maple syrup
60g coconut oil, melted
200ml fresh lime juice (about 10 limes)
2 tsp vanilla extract
Pinch of sea salt
Zest of 1 lime

Grease a 20cm round springform tin with oil. Put all the base ingredients into a food processor and blitz until the mixture is finely ground and sticks together when pressed between your fingers. Press very firmly into the base and sides of the tin to make an even and smooth crust. Cover and refrigerate for 30 minutes, or place in the freezer for 15 minutes, until set.

Put all the topping ingredients, except the lime zest, into a food processor and blitz for a few minutes until completely smooth and creamy. Pour the mixture over the base and put it back in the fridge to set for at least 2–3 hours or overnight. Alternatively, put the pie in the freezer for 45 minutes and then transfer it to the fridge.

When ready to serve, carefully transfer the tart on to a serving dish and scatter over the lime zest. You can keep this in the fridge in an airtight container for up to 3 days.

"

I THINK COOKING SHOULD BE FUN, BECAUSE THAT'S THE BEST WAY TO PASS ON ALL THE TRICKS AND SKILLS FROM ONE GENERATION TO THE NEXT.

"

Linda McCartney — 1989

COCONUT RICE PUDDING

Coconut milk makes a beautifully creamy rice pudding and the vanilla extract lifts the flavour perfectly. Serve with whatever fresh fruit you like, but mango does go well with the coconut and brings a refreshingly tropical feel to this family favourite.

SERVES 4–6

150g short-grain rice

400ml tin of coconut milk

800ml unsweetened, plant-based milk of your choice

85g unrefined sugar or golden caster sugar

Pinch of sea salt

1 tsp vanilla extract

60g desiccated coconut (optional)

To serve

Slices of mango or other seasonal fruit, such as strawberries or raspberries

Toasted coconut flakes

Put the rice, coconut milk, plant milk, sugar and a pinch of salt into a large saucepan and bring to the boil. Reduce the heat a little and simmer briskly for 20 minutes, stirring frequently.

Add the vanilla and the desiccated coconut, if using, and simmer for another 5 minutes, stirring regularly, until thick and creamy.

Serve hot or cold with slices of fresh fruit and some toasted coconut flakes scattered over the top.

ETON MESS

Aquafaba is a little touch of culinary magic. It is the liquid you find in a tin of chickpeas and, when whisked, it takes on the consistency and appearance of beaten egg whites. And, like them, it can be used to make meringues for this divine English pudding. If you don't want to use the chickpeas on the same day, freeze them for another time.

SERVES 6

100ml aquafaba, the
    drained liquid from a tin
    of unsalted chickpeas
½ tsp cream of tartar or
    white wine vinegar
100g unrefined or
    caster sugar
½ tsp vanilla extract

To serve
600g strawberries, hulled
    and roughly chopped
1 tbsp unrefined or
    caster sugar
600g coconut or
    soya yoghurt
Fresh mint leaves (optional)

Preheat the oven to 120°C/Fan 100°C/Gas ½ and line a large baking tray with baking paper.

Put the aquafaba and the cream of tartar or vinegar into the bowl of a stand mixer and whisk until thick and glossy and soft peaks begin to form. A handheld electric whisk can also be used for this.

Gradually add the sugar a tablespoon at a time while whisking on high speed, ensuring each spoon of sugar is fully incorporated before adding the next. Add in the vanilla and continue to whisk for another 2–4 minutes until the meringue forms stiff peaks and is glossy, thick and holds its shape. You should be able to turn the bowl upside down without the meringue falling out.

Transfer the meringue into a piping bag and pipe 5cm rounds on to the tray. Alternatively, you can use 2 spoons. Bake in the oven for 90 minutes, making sure not to open the oven at any point. Turn off the oven and leave the door closed for a further hour, then remove and leave to cool completely. Once cool, transfer to an airtight container and refrigerate until needed. Don't worry if they begin to crack.

When ready to serve, put a third of the strawberries into a food processor or blender and blitz down to a sauce. Transfer the sauce to a bowl with the remaining strawberries and fold through one tablespoon of sugar. Layer the yoghurt, strawberry mixture and meringues into 6 glasses, breaking them up as you go in order to fit, and top with a sprig of mint if you like. Serve immediately.

STRAWBERRY CHEESECAKE

A real showstopper, this fabulous cheesecake has a rich, creamy strawberry filling on a crisp almond and date base. Ideally, the cashew nuts for the cheesecake filling should be soaked overnight first, but don't panic if you forget. Just chop the nuts roughly, cook them in a pan of boiling water for 15 minutes, then drain, cool and proceed as below.

SERVES 10–12

Base

140g flavourless coconut oil, melted

60g raw unsalted almonds

80g oatcakes

80g pitted medjool dates

Pinch of sea salt

Filling

350g strawberries, hulled, plus extra to decorate

160g unrefined or caster sugar

400g raw unsalted cashew nuts, soaked overnight in cold water

Grated zest of 2 unwaxed lemons and 1 tbsp juice

70g non-dairy plain yoghurt or oat cream

1 tsp vanilla extract

½ tsp sea salt

To serve

Extra strawberries

Fresh mint leaves

Grease a 20cm round springform cake tin with a little of the oil. For the base, put the almonds, oatcakes, dates, 2 tablespoons of the melted coconut oil and a pinch of salt into the bowl of a food processor. Blitz until everything is very finely ground and sticks together when pressed between your fingers. Firmly press the mixture into the greased cake tin. Place in the freezer for about 15 minutes to set.

For the cheesecake, put the 350g of strawberries and the sugar into a saucepan and place over a medium heat. Squash the berries with the back of a spoon to release their liquid, and bring to simmering point, stirring frequently, until the sugar has dissolved. Leave to simmer for 2 minutes, then remove the pan from the heat and leave to cool.

Meanwhile, drain the cashew nuts and blitz them to a smooth paste in a food processor or high-speed blender. Add the remaining melted coconut oil, the lemon zest and juice, yoghurt or cream, vanilla, salt and the cooled strawberry and sugar mixture. Blitz again until completely smooth – it may take a few minutes to achieve this. Pour the mixture over the set base and smooth out. Cover and return to the freezer for at least 5 hours or preferably overnight.

Before serving, remove the cheesecake from the freezer and leave to thaw for 30–45 minutes, or until you can cut into the cake without too much resistance. Serve with more strawberries on top and some sprigs of mint. This cheesecake is best stored in the freezer, but remove it 30–45 minutes before serving.

PLUM COBBLER

A recipe inspired by Linda's American heritage, a cobbler is a traditional dessert similar to a crumble but with a scrumptious, scone-like topping. You can use all kinds of seasonal fruit, but we particularly enjoy this plum version, flavoured with hints of lemon, cinnamon and vanilla. Aromatic and luscious.

SERVES 8

120g coconut oil, plus extra to grease

150g white spelt or plain flour

50g ground almonds

200g unrefined or caster sugar

2 tsp baking powder

¾ tsp fine sea salt

130ml soya or oat cream

800g plums, stones removed and cut into quarters

Zest of 1 unwaxed lemon

1 tsp vanilla extract

1 tsp ground cinnamon

1½ tbsp cornflour

To serve

Non-dairy ice cream or yoghurt

Preheat the oven to 200°C/Fan 180°C/Gas 6 and grease a large pie dish with coconut oil.

In a large bowl, mix together the flour, ground almonds, 70g of the sugar, the baking powder and salt. Rub in the coconut oil until the mixture resembles fine breadcrumbs, then pour in the cream and combine to form a wet dough.

Put the quartered plums in a large bowl and combine with the remaining sugar (keep back a tablespoon for sprinkling on top), the lemon zest, vanilla extract, cinnamon and cornflour. Transfer to the pie dish, then place heaped tablespoons of the dough on top of the fruit, positioning the mounds in neat rows. Sprinkle the reserved tablespoon of sugar over the cobbler topping.

Bake for 35–40 minutes, until deeply golden brown and bubbling. Leave to cool for 10–15 minutes, then serve with ice cream or yoghurt.

*M*y mum truly was the heart of our home, so this meant that we gravitated to wherever she was. Mostly we found ourselves in the kitchen, sitting around the table – shouting, singing, laughing, screaming, crying. Everything happened in the kitchen, and warmth and love radiated from there throughout the house. Mum had an amazing way of making food that brought people together, no matter what she cooked. You could feel the love that she had put into the preparation of a meal. I remember Mum saying that cooking is the ultimate art form. You spend so many hours toiling over a hot stove – peeling, chopping, sieving, frying, stirring, grating – then in seconds it's gobbled up and gone. Eating together as a family is one of my most precious memories.

Another thing I find amazing about Mum is that she really did do all the cooking for our family – something I think might come as a surprise to a lot of people, considering the privileged life we had. Mum could have had any cook she wanted making meals for her, but I truly think that she enjoyed the role of wife and mother and knew the importance of providing well-cooked, well-loved nutritional food for her husband, children and herself.

Stella

CASHEW, COCONUT AND CHOCOLATE SQUARES

These taste like guilty pleasures, but actually all the ingredients are nutritious. There's no real cooking involved, other than melting the oil and chocolate, and when the mixture is made you just leave it in the fridge or freezer to set. Simple and utterly delicious.

MAKES 16 SQUARES

100g desiccated coconut, plus extra for topping

200g pitted medjool dates

130g raw unsalted cashew nuts

3 tbsp coconut oil, melted

1 tsp ground cinnamon

Large pinch of sea salt

70g dark chocolate

Line a 20cm square baking tin with baking paper.

Put all the ingredients, except the chocolate, into a food processor and blitz until everything is ground down and comes together into a sticky ball.

Press the mixture firmly into the lined baking tin and smooth out with the back of a spoon. A layer of cling film placed over the surface helps prevent the spoon from sticking to the mixture.

Cover and refrigerate for 1–2 hours or place in the freezer for about 30 minutes, until very well chilled and set.

Break up the chocolate and put it in a heatproof bowl placed over a pan of barely simmering water. Make sure the bottom of the bowl doesn't touch the water. Stir the chocolate every now and again until it has melted.

Remove the baking tin from the fridge or freezer and pour over the melted chocolate, working very quickly to smooth it out before it sets. Scatter over a little more desiccated coconut and leave the chocolate to set.

Once set, cut into 16 squares of equal size. To achieve a clean cut on the chocolate layer, simply dip a long sharp knife into boiling water and pat dry before cutting. Store in an airtight container and keep in the fridge for up to 3 weeks.

RESOURCES

The following websites include further information on plant-based eating and the protection of animals and the environment.

FOOD AND FARMING

British Dietetic Association – includes fact sheets on healthy plant-based eating.
www.bda.uk.com

Meat Free Monday – a not-for-profit campaign which aims to raise awareness of the detrimental environmental impact of animal agriculture and industrial fishing, as well as encourage plant-based eating.
www.meatfreemondays.com

Movement for Compassionate Living – aims to spread the vegan message and promote vegan organic farming and local production.
www.mclveganway.org.uk

Vegan Directory UK – an online guide to vegan businesses and organisations in the UK.

www.vegandirectory.uk

Vegan Society – information about how to adopt a vegan lifestyle, with recipes, advice and latest news.
www.vegansociety.com

Vegetarian Society – information about the vegetarian way of eating, including nutritional advice and recipes.
www.vegsoc.org

Viva! – a leading vegan campaigning charity, aiming to create a kinder and more sustainable world for animals and humans.
www.viva.org.uk

ANIMAL WELFARE

Animal Aid – campaigns peacefully against animal use and promotes a cruelty-free lifestyle.

www.animalaid.org.uk

CAFT (Coalition to Abolish the Fur Trade) – investigates and lobbies against the fur trade.
www.caft.org.uk

Compassion in world farming (CIWF) – campaigns to end all factory farming.
www.ciwf.org.uk

Peta (People for the Ethical Treatment of Animals) – the largest animal rights organisation in the world.
www.peta.org

Uncaged – campaigns against animal testing and experiments.
www.uncaged.co.uk

World Animal Protection – campaigns worldwide for animal welfare and an end to animal cruelty.
www.worldanimalprotection.org.uk

ENVIRONMENT

The Climate Coalition – dedicated to action against climate change and to working for a cleaner, greener world.
www.theclimatecoalition.org

The Climate Group – campaigns internationally to drive climate action, with a goal of world net zero carbon emissions by 2050.
www.theclimategroup.org

Friends of the Earth – dedicated to protecting the natural world and the wellbeing of everyone in it.
www.friendsoftheearth.uk

Greenpeace – campaigns on planet-saving issues such as climate change, deforestation, overfishing and whaling.
www.greenpeace.org.uk

First published in Great Britain in 2021 by Seven Dials
An imprint of The Orion Publishing Group Ltd
Carmelite House, 50 Victoria Embankment
London, EC4Y 0DZ
An Hachette UK Company

10 9 8 7 6 5 4 3 2 1

Introduction, recipes, additional text and illustrations
© Linda Enterprises Ltd

A CIP catalogue record for this book
is available from the British Library.

ISBN (Hardback): 978 1 8418 8363 2
ISBN (eBook): 978 1 84188364 9

Publisher: Anna Valentine
Project editor: Jinny Johnson
Recipe development by Jordan Bourke with the McCartney family
Illustrator: Stina Persson
Production: Nicole Abel
Photography: Issy Croker
Food styling: Emily Ezekiel
Thanks to: Alex Parker, Andrea Parton, Annie Mordue, Anya Hassett, Grace Guppy,
Issy Bingham, Kim Panter, Laura Eastman Malcolm, Lee Eastman, Louise Morris, Louise
Weed, Richard Ewbank, Richard Miller, Sam Merry, Sarah Brown, Steve Ithell, Tina Deane

Printed and bound in Italy by L.E.G.O. S.p.A.

MIX
Paper from
responsible sources
FSC® C023419
www.fsc.org

Note: While every effort has been made to ensure
that the information in this book is correct, it should
not be substituted for medical advice. It is the sole
responsibility of the reader to determine which foods
are safe to consume. If you are concerned about any
aspect of your health, speak to your GP.

LindaMcCartney.com
LindaMcCartneyFoods.co.uk
www.orionbooks.co.uk